Dear Axel…

Dear Axel...

99 Postcards from
Alison and Peter Smithson

Anna Bach

For Karlchen.

First published by
Verlag der Buchhandlung Walther und Franz König
Ehrenstrasse 4
D-50672 Cologne, Germany
verlag@buchhandlung-walther-koenig.de

Bibliographical information published by the Deutsche Nationalbibliothek.
The Deutsche Nationalbibliothek lists this publication in the Deutsche Nationalbibliographie; detailed bibliographic data are available online at http://dnb.d-nd.de.

Editor: Moisés Puente
Graphic Design: RafamateoStudio
Proofreading: George Hutton
Printing: AS Printon

© of the texts: their authors
© Verlag der Buchhandlung Walther und Franz König, Cologne, 2025

Printed in Estonia
ISBN: 978-3-7533-0900-2

99 Postcards

Anna Bach

Between 1985 and 2002, the British architects Alison and Peter Smithson transformed the Hexenhaus — a little, half-timbered building, nestled in a Grimm fairy tale-like forest in Bad Karlshafen, Germany — from a modest vernacular cottage to one of the most remarkable houses of the late twentieth century. The architects completely redefined the relationship between the house and its surrounding landscape by means of more than twenty small additions, extractions, satellite buildings, furnishing operations and alternative routes. During this long process, they established a close relationship with their client, Axel Bruchhäuser, who still lives in the Hexenhaus to this day. Axel is a key figure when it comes to comprehending the house's design. As Peter Smithson wrote: "To work with such a person is to receive notions, strongly felt and expressed, which are the beginning of a spatial transformation. Each gives what the other needs."[1]

The Hexenhaus is more than a house. It is a living organism adapting to the life of those who live there, namely a man and his cat. This adaptation is essential, not only to improve the physical living environment, but also to provide a context that allows for the continuous re-interpretation of the house. The Hexenhaus is an instrument that enables meaningful interaction between its inhabitants and its architects. A static, solid building becomes a dynamic and ever-changing catalyst for human relation.

Both Alison and Peter Smithson were prolific writers, and their texts make up a vital component of their *oeuvre*. The Smithsons considered the act of writing to be a natural part of being an architect. They tended to write short articles on their own work and thinking, but also addressing a wide range of questions about the profession, society, nature and so on, with titles such as "In "In Praise of Cupboard Doors", "Collective Design: The Good-tempered Gas Man" or "But Today We Collect Ads".[2] Their texts are seemingly spontaneous, though they were frequently corrected, edited, revised and even re-written. Nevertheless, they conserve a particular freshness and brevity, and are often constructed around one thought or idea.

Alison and Peter wrote separately, though some of their texts have been published as joint works under both of their names.

The authorship was usually indicated by the initials AS or PS, but even without these signatures, it would be evident who the writer was; they were each interested in different themes, and had their own style. Peter's writing was more closely concerned with architecture and its tangible qualities, albeit sometimes in a very poetic manner. Alison's writing was complex and had more registers.[3] Her texts are often hard to follow as the writing seems to be even more spontaneous than Peter's, verging on stream-of-consciousness. On the other hand, Alison was the one who used to note the meticulous minutes of meetings in the studio, and was an active letter-writer. She was the one who kept in touch with clients, colleagues, editorials, universities etc.

Something similar happened with the Smithsons' architectural projects, insomuch that two distinct authors invariably presented as one unit. The Hexenhaus interventions were originally Alison's work, while Peter was busy designing the new buildings for the University of Bath. The plans for Axel's Porch, the Riverbank Window and the Hexenhaus Holes are all signed by Alison, who passed away in 1993 after having completed the detailed drawings for one more intervention — the Hexenbesenraum.[4] This watchtower-like construction was particularly ambitious and mysterious. Its tower stands apart from the original house, and is not a modification or an extension; instead, it offers an experience of leaving the initial building, entering the tree tops and looking back to the house and its surrounding nature, from distance. After Alison's death, Peter and Axel had a serious conversation about the legitimacy of carrying on Alison's work for the house, and they concluded that the project should continue. Peter went on to design nineteen further modifications, including a revised version of the Hexenbesenraum, which was finally built in 1995.

During the years of work on the Hexenhaus, the correspondence between the architects and their client was intense. It is worth remembering that, in the 1980s and 90s, the most common form of international communication was by post. This might seem obvious, but it really is a far cry from the immediacy that we now live in. The postal service has its specific formats and time delays: ideas, thoughts or orders can easily take a week to travel from one interlocutor to the other. Letters permit a considerable amount of information, but everything has to fit into an envelope, and extra weight comes with an additional cost. Postcards are more compact — perhaps comparable with a text (or voice message!) of today. The space is reduced to just one side of a 10 × 15 cm piece of card, which is further diminished by the address lines and the area taken up by the stamp. Alison wrote many letters, and the Hexenhaus project needed a means of communication that would shorten the distance between Cato Lodge — their London residence and office — and the Hexenhaus in Bad Karlshafen. The minutes of meetings travelled together with plans and descriptions, and very often a postcard would be slipped into the package. These postcards would be jammed full of text and sketches, making the most of their flexibility as a format. When sending a postcard within a larger package (which already contained the address information, airmail label and stamps) Alison in particular would often use the whole surface, sometimes even the picture side. The Smithsons would send independent postcards too, without a package or envelope, and these were equally tightly written in order to take full advantage of the limited available area; the final parts often snaked around the postcard, to use up any remaining gaps. The advantage of postcards was, and still is, that they are less formal than letters. Their picture side adds another layer of information that can be used to exchange visual references, a little wink that might refer to the ongoing exchange of ideas or as a way to share the imaginary from a trip.

There is no record of the postcards or letters that Axel Bruchhäuser wrote to the Smithsons. It seems that the postcards travelled mostly from the UK to Germany, and much less in the other direction. Axel does not share the Smithsons' passion for writing, and the use of English makes him even more reluctant. Axel has saved just under a hundred postcards written by Alison and Peter, originally stored as a part of the Hexenhaus miscellanea — on top of shelves, on the writing desk, under a pile of books, pinned onto the wall, and so on. In 2018, I got the chance to gather them all together, organise them and, more importantly, read them! According to a somewhat exaggerated comment by Axel, I am the only person in the world who has ever read all the Smithsons' postcards — he claims that he did not always have the time or patience to do so as and when they arrived. Since then, the idea to share this peculiar one-sided correspondence has been on my mind.

In this collection, there are 55 postcards written by Alison and 44 by Peter. Before Alison passed away, Peter hardly ever wrote to Axel. He only really started to send cards when he knew that Alison was seriously ill. Peter took over Alison's tasks for the Hexenhaus, both as an architect and as a friend who kept in contact with the client. The Smithsons' postcards illustrate the difference between the two authors. The first clear difference is quantitative: the postcards from Alison contain more than 4,200 words in total, whereas Peter uses only around 1,300 words in his. Alison's messages are densely written in tight handwriting, whereas Peter's take up just a few lines and are usually in all-capital letters. Perhaps because Alison was the one who began the relationship with the client, her writing is more formal than Peter's; for example, her postcards begin "Dear Axel", whereas Peter tends to use a simple "Axel!". Furthermore, Alison's messages indicate a professional relationship with the client, as they are written in order to organise meetings, the shipping of catalogues, the fabrication of prototypes, trips, ongoing tasks and ideas for future projects. Their growing friendship is hidden behind the shared passion for work. By the time of Alison's death, the Smithsons had been involved with Axel for more than ten years, and perhaps that is why Peter's messages are somewhat less formal. His postcards contain friendly comments on shared interests or ongoing projects, but they are rarely used as means of professional exchange of information. Measurements, material descriptions or other data cannot be found in these postcards. Much of the professional information was transferred during the on-site visits, or in writing issue notes together with drawings. The passage of time and the ever-closer relationship does not fully explain the differences of tone in the writing, though. Alison and Peter had two very different styles of communicating with the people around them; Alison was somewhat distant though very intense, and Peter was more tranquil, with a subtle, slightly sarcastic sense of humour.

Many of the postcards contain ideas for furniture, with comments on specific finishing materials or details. Some even have material samples stapled onto them. Axel Bruchhäuser, as a manufacturer of innovative design furniture,[5] first became interested in the Smithsons for their furniture designs, such as the Trundling Turk lounge chair from 1953 and the Red Boxes originally made for the Economist Building in 1968. The Smithsons were introduced to Bruchhäuser through their common friend, the artist, designer and architect Stefan Wewerka,[6] and from the early 1980s Alison worked on around fifteen furniture designs for Bruchhäuser's firm Tecta. Many of these were used in exhibitions as prototypes or manufactured for the Hexenhaus, but only a few were ever brought into commercial production, for economical and/or technical reasons. Alison's postcards were often triggered by visits to museums or furniture exhibitions, where she would source ideas and solutions for Tecta. A postcard from 1988 shows Alison's true dedication to this task: "You can see to what effort I go to investigate boxes: how they can be attached and what to put in them." She continues: "Maybe there could be a Tecta treasure box where each of your artists / collaborators fill one compartment with a special object: made of wood."[7] Subsequently, in the late 1990s, Peter designed more furniture for the firm, most importantly the Popova lattice furniture and the latticed screen. The postcard sent in November 1997, which has just the word "branching" on it, is a message alluding to the formal language of these items. The concepts of branching and lattice were clearly related to the contemporaneous interventions on the Hexenhaus. If writing was considered a natural part of being an architect, then so was designing furniture.

The Smithsons' travels, during the years of their collaboration on the Hexenhaus, were another cause for sending postcards. They would write to Axel from far-away locations, on their various kind of trips, such as for lecturing, exhibitions or family holidays. It is easy to imagine the writing happening in airport halls or in hotel rooms and lobbies. Alison and Peter had a busy travel agenda from the 1980s onwards; Alison was teaching abroad — first in Delft (1983-84), then in Cologne (1985) and later in Barcelona (1986) — whereas Peter spent a couple of weeks every summer (from 1977 to 2001) at the ILA&UD summer school[8] in Urbino, Siena or Venice. Aside from these teaching visits, they also travelled to China, the Soviet Union, the United States, Singapore, South Africa, Greece, Sweden, Switzerland, Turkey, France... and the postcards kept on turning up at Bad Karlshafen.

The Hexenhaus itself is mentioned in only a few of the postcards. The one dated May 1985 is clearly a "working postcard", dealing with the first intervention of Axel's Porch.[9] It is sent from Singapore, and asks for the exact measurements of the existing garden doors, which were recycled in the new porch. The postcard includes a sketch in plan of the doors, clarifying which measurements are needed. Another postcard from 1990 expresses Alison's desire to "see the changed & changing light quality in your house"[10] after completing the Hexenhaus Holes, which brought light to the back of the living room and visually connected the two floors of the house. Peter writes in the early 2000s with an idea for "another use for Lantern Pavilion! 'Actors' inside / audience outside...".[11] One postcard from 2002 deals with the Front Door Porch.[12] And that is it — the Hexenhaus appears in just four postcards! This is not entirely the case, though; even if the house doesn't appear as a specific subject or project, the life in it seeps into most of the messages. Karlchen, Bruchhäuser's cat, is the link to the everyday life in the Hexenhaus, and he often receives a special greeting from both Alison and Peter.

Alison and Peter Smithson's postcards may not necessarily reveal more about the architecture itself of the Hexenhaus, but they certainly illustrate the close relationship between the architects and their dear client, bearing witness to the continuous contact and collaboration that went on for almost twenty years. A tender message from 2001 beautifully illustrates the complicity between them: "We have to hang-on to each other, for we are only few."[13]

The postcards are ordered chronologically, though organised by author; first the ones written by Alison, and then the ones by Peter. This does not alter the overall chronology substantially, as Peter wrote most of his postcards after Alison had passed away. Some of the cards are undated. This is the case, especially, with many of Alison's postcards (17 of them) and fewer of Peter's (4). The lack of date or postal stamp is due to the fact that Alison's postcards would often arrive as part of a pack with other material, or enclosed in envelopes that have since been discarded. An effort has been made to situate the messages in time. There are a couple of even more mysterious postcards — one from Alison that is dated a year after her death, and one that arrived before the relationship with Axel Bruchhäuser had even started!

The transcription has followed the original texts as faithfully as possible; the use of upper or lower cases and special characters has been respected, and spelling mistakes have not been corrected. It has been impossible to decode some of the words, or they may have been interpreted incorrectly. The editor's comments are in red. They sometimes describe sketches, stapled pieces of paper or other material that is not in text form. Some comments help clarify the context, or they attempt to pinpoint when certain postcards were sent, if the date is absent or ambiguous.

Alongside the transcription, the two sides of the postcards are shown together, because the written message and the image often complete each other. Some card designs are repeated, which indicates that the Smithsons occasionally bought a pile of postcards they liked and then used them later on. The repetition is obvious with their own postcards, which they had made for the office. The images on the cards can be divided into four rough groups:

1. The first and largest group contains "museum postcards" that depict furniture throughout history, from vernacular chairs to Victorian cabinets and Bauhaus classics, as well as works of fine art. There are plenty of medieval and early-Renaissance art cards: it seems that the Smithsons were interested in the architectonic scenography of these paintings, furnished as they were with canopies, arches, pedestals and cabinets, being used by kings, saints or even tax collectors. The oak frame with the head of St John in gilded alabaster almost forms a room in itself.[14] Alison wrote on top of the image "I like the sauna". One imagines that she was not referring to the cut-off head, but rather to the furniture-like space creating a dense atmosphere. Art from the early twentieth century also features strongly, particularly works by El Lissitzky. This was not only because Alison and Peter were interested in the Russian artist, but because Axel was very interested in this kind of kinetic art. In the Tecta collection there are various items by El Lissitzky, and Axel reinterpreted some of his graphic artworks as sculptural objects that are now in the Hexenhaus, together with a selection of original prints. The thirties are notably present in this group too, given the Smithsons' common interest in both the design and the architecture that emerged during that decade. As they wrote in the in-

troduction of their book *The 1930's* (1985): "Our sensibility towards the work of the period has been heightened over the last three or four years by working contact with the furniture manufacturer Axel Bruchhäuser of Lauenförde."[15]

2. Another clear group is what we might call "tourist postcards". They represent the postcards available to the Smithsons at hotels, airports and centric locations, i.e. places where it would be easy to find stamps and a post box. These postcards are iconic images of historical buildings or monuments, beautiful (somewhat kitsch) landscapes or other clichés of the tourist imaginary; a bullfighting arena from Barcelona, a turquoise beach with a man riding a donkey from Greece, teepees and the Golden Gate Bridge from the United States... These pictures reflect the subtle sense of humour of the Smithsons.

3. In this same sense, we can also separate out a third group of postcards, depicting "random oddities". Among other visual allusions, we can find historical machines such as heaters, sewing machines or engines, which seem to have drawn the attention of the Smithsons. They probably assumed that Axel, as an engineer, would be interested in them too.

4. Finally, a few cards feature the Smithsons' own designs, such as illustrations for the Parc de la Villette competition entry from 1982, or the invitation to their 1992 exhibition at b.d, Madrid, for which the waterlily and fish axonometry were professionally printed as postcards. Another type of card was produced in the office as well: Alison and Peter used small drawings, symbols and signs as part of their thinking process for projects, whether buildings, furniture or writing. Sometimes, at some point of the drawing and redrawing, the sign gained independence and was transformed into a symbol. Then, some of these symbols were used as an image or stamp for the studio. Alison herself lino-printed them on 10 × 15 cm cards, which were then used as notes to slip between books to be sent out, or as postcards. It seems that Ron Simpson, a good friend of the architects, kept his printing press at the Gilston Road office, which was used by the Smithsons. These postcards were readily available at the studio, so were used repeatedly. Some other images seemed to

warrant being reused as well; the Apollo Electric Fireplace postcard appears a couple of times, as does the card with St John's Head and the Tetrarchs. Given that The Smithsons were such active postcard writers, if they found one they liked, then they would buy several of them so that they would always have some at hand when needed.

---

1 Smithson, Peter, "Being at Home", Venice: *ILA&UD Yearbook – Territory and Identity* 1, 1997.

2 Smithson, Peter, "In Praise of Cupboard Doors", in Van den Heuvel, Dirk and Risselada, Max (eds.), *From the House of the Future to the House of Today*, Rotterdam: 010 Publishers, 2004; Smithson, Alison, "Collective Design: The Good-tempered Gas Man", *Architectural Design*, London, March 1975; and "But Today We Collect Ads', *Ark*, no. 18, London, November 1956.

3 Alison Smithson even wrote and published a novel called *A Portrait of the Female Mind as a Young Girl*, London: Chatto & Windus, 1966.

4 "Hexenbesenraum" means the "Room for the Witches' Brooms". Wordplay and references to the Brothers Grimm and other popular German fairytales is a constant in the Hexenhaus/Tecta projects. See, for example, the Struwwelpeter Cabinet and the Tischlein deck dich table.

5 Axel Bruchhäuser's furniture company, Tecta, specialised in producing many of the Bauhaus designs, as well as furniture designed by Jean Prouvé, Stefan Wewerka and the Smithsons.

6 One postcard to Stefan Wewerka (pp. 16-17) has been included in the collection, as he was closely collaborating with Axel and Tecta. This postcard eventually led to the meeting of all four — Alison, Peter, Axel and Stefan — at the Tecta factory in Lauenförde, later in 1984.

7 See postcard pp. 62-63.

8 The Italian architect Giancarlo De Carlo ran ILA&UD (International Laboratory for Architecture and Urban Design) from 1976 onwards, in various locations in Italy.

9 See postcard pp. 28-29.

10 See postcard pp. 96-97, probably from 1990.

11 See postcard pp. 194-195, probably from 2000-01.

12 See postcard pp. 208-209.

13 See postcard pp. 188-189.

14 See postcards pp- 72-73 and 74-75.

15 Smithson, Alison and Peter, *The 1930's*, Berlin: Tecta/Alexander Verlag, 1985.

Editor's Note:
The transcriptions of the postcards written by Alison and Peter Smithson appear in black, while Anna Bach's comments are in red.

© Anna Bach, 2018

99 Postcards

Morecambe Pier
© *Clive Frost from 'Dreamland'*
Sims & Frost

Dear Stefan, April 2/84
I think we have 'missed the boat' as far as the joint photograph with Jean Prouvé is concerned .... - what now? Do you still exhibit in Paris? Somehow we must all - Axel included in this - meet up somewhere and drink some wine to Prouvé and the furniture.
Our regards to all. Alison.
Telephone us if you go to Paris and are making the exhibition.

THE POSTCARD GALLERY PRINTED IN ENGLAND BY RENSHURST PRESS

Alison Smithson, 2 April 1984

April 2/84

Dear Stefan,
I think we have 'missed the boat' as far as the joint photograph with Jean Prouvé is concerned.... — what now? Do you still exhibit in Paris? Somehow we must all — Axel included in this — meet up somewhere and drink some wine to Prouvé and the furniture.
Our regards to all.
Alison
Telephone us if you go to Paris and are making the exhibition.

The postcard is directed to Stefan Wewerka, Tecta's creative director from the late 1970s. Wewerka was the person who first introduced the Smithsons to Axel Bruchhäuser in the early 1980s, and he acted as a middle-man between the client and the architects.
Axel, Stefan and the Smithsons had been planning a trip to Paris in order to meet Jean Prouvé, but he died on March 23, 1984. Their Paris rendezvous was thus cancelled and instead organized at Tecta in Lauenförde, Germany.

DANCING
SKATING

THE MINIMAL CELLA POSTCARD
for Cellawoman?

(actually, the cella should either unfold from this size of 'thing' or be simply 'another level'; as simple and elegant as the Imam's seat in the Hasan Mosque, Cairo

Ron Simpson's Bat chair

also sent on van for appraisal of actual object. I would like to see a silver see-through 'net' or fabric as the seat. attached 'solar' samples probably too thin but this is area for search (150cms wide)
These are VEROSOL samples made in Holland, distributed here by Fromberg Agency.

No. 50: "ALL IN GOOD TIME: SELF PORTRAIT BOX" by Jo Bondy
Wood and Mixed Media. 186 × 37 × 27 cms. 1981.
Nicholas Treadwell Gallery, London

Nicholas Treadwell Publications

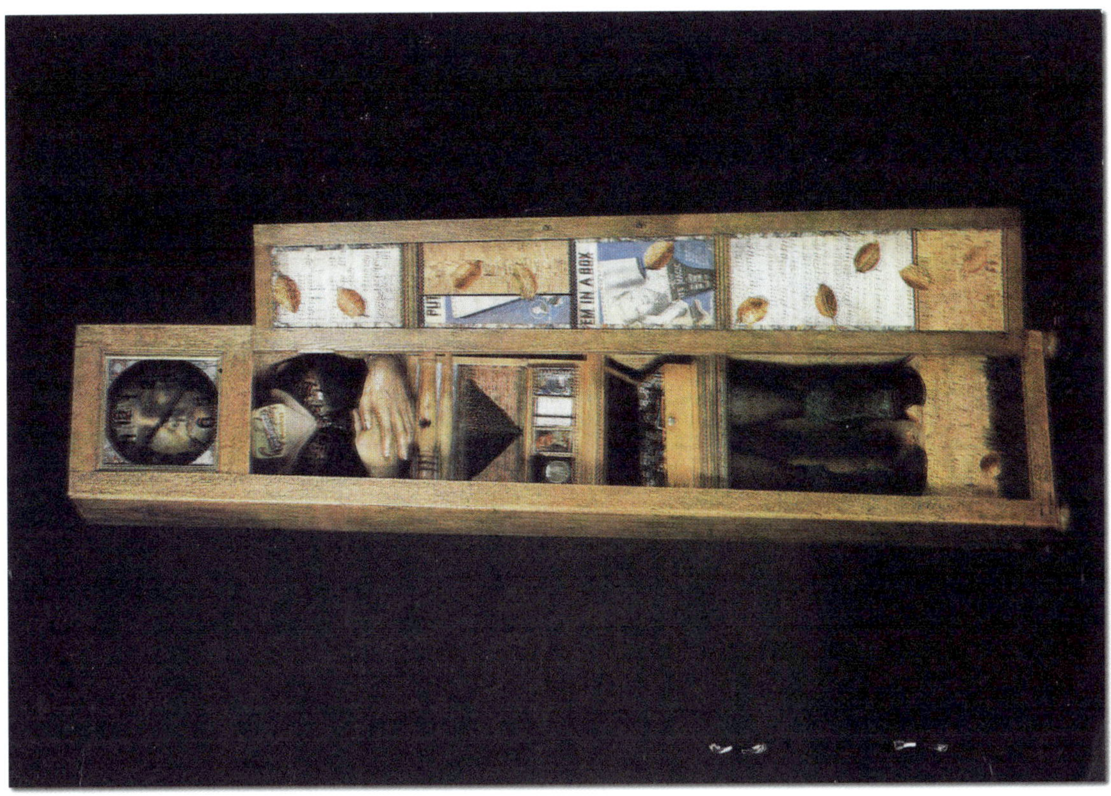

Alison Smithson, undated / circa 1984

THE MINIMAL CELLA POSTCARD
for Cellawoman? (actually, the cella should either unfold from this size of 'thing' or be simply 'another level'; as simple and elegant as the Imam's seat in the Hassan Mosque, Cairo.

[A drawing depicting the Imam's chair]

Ron Simpson's Bat chair also sent on van for apraisal of actual object. I would like to see a silver see-through 'net' or fabric as the seat. Attached 'solar' samples probably too thin but this is area for search.
These are VEROSOL samples (150 cm wide) made in Holland, distributed here by Fromberg Agency.

[Two silver-grey fabric samples glued onto the edge of the postcard]

Unsigned.

The postcard is likely to be from 1983-84. At that time, Alison was teaching at TU Delft in the Netherlands, and the Cella project by Stefan Wewerka for Tecta was published in 1984.

London 25 June 84

Dear Axel,
Thank you very much
for the chair (Stefan's?) that
arrived as a surprise in a
Tecta carton. We are not sure
where your factory is – near
Hamburg?– we will enquire of
the possibility of breaking our
flight en route sometime to
Munich if the plans are fulfilled
for us to visit as professors
1984-85. Alison M Smithson

tel. G.Road London 2351317 D31

Peter and Alison Smithson
Parc de la Villette 1982

Published by Manspace Gallery and the Building Centre 1984

Alison Smithson, 25 June 1984

London 25 June 84

Dear Axel,
Thank you very much for the chair (Stefan's?) that arrived as a surprise in a Tecta carton. We are not sure where your factory is — near Hamburg? — we will enquire of the possibility of breaking our flight en route sometime to Munich if the plans are fulfilled for us to visit as professors 1984-85.
Alison M Smithson
[Note at the side, probably by Axel]:
tel. G.Road London 2351317 [?] D31

[Text below the image]: Cow pasture with a bronze herd of Charolais standing in lush looking meadow grass in which buttercups are allowed to grow before the first cut. Beech hedges contain purple sycamores; the free-standing specimen trees are willows (set against hornbeam hedges) and copper beeches. To the east the pyrocanthus clothed cone that conceals the globe; its facetted top contains observatories for armatures.
AMS February 2/81

24 Gilston Road, London S.W.10
9SR.
November 21st 1984

Dear Tecta,
Thank you very much for having me to stay and visit with you in Bad Karlshafen to see the factory and discuss things.... and leave by train.
I will write you soon the detail comments on some of the things spoken about, together with some drawings
Kindest regards
Alison M Smithson

Alison Smithson, 21 November 1984

24 Gilston Road,
London S.W.10 9SR.
November 21st 1984

Dear Tecta,
Thank you very much for having me to stay and visit with you in Bad Karlshafen to see the factory and discuss things… and leave by train.
I will write you soon the detail comments on some of the things spoken about, together with some drawings

Kindest regards
Alison M Smithson

Written after Alison's first visit to Tecta. Until then, Alison Smithson and Tecta had collaborated from distance. The Smithsons' personal relationship with Axel had not quite been established yet, and therefore the postcard is addressed impersonally to Tecta. The first visit together with Peter took place in March 1985. That is when Alison and Peter, Stefan Wewerka and Axel Bruchhäuser met all together for the first time.

Alison Smithson, undated / circa 1984

Dear Axel: Could you please send a chair catalogue to
MAX RISSELADA
TU DELFT
FACULTEIT DER BOUWKUNDE
BERLAGEWEG 1
2628 CR DELFT
THE NETHERLANDS
I tell you why, he has made 5 models of Prouvé houses. He is very interested in Prouvé (among many other things) & thinks the office I visited in Paris of Prouvé might have been at the road side going out of Neuilly to La Défense by CEMT factory he worked with: could you ask his family for the Paris office address(es) please and I will go and look next time I am there & see if there is anything.

ARCHITECTURE VIVANTE/Ed Badovici/Morance/Paris
1930/ Tranvieri Club, Moscow/Melnikov, 1929

[written vertically, referring to the five models]:
Maybe they could be loaned for an exhibition?
[written vertically]:
Max said the El Lissitzky is called SKY IRONER in English.

Alison and Peter Smithson taught at TU Delft in Holland in 1983-84, with Max Risselada as their assistant. Later on, Risselada was professor of architectural design at TU Delft, and he is author of several studies, exhibitions and publications on the Smithsons.

ALISON & PETER SMITHSON CATO LODGE 24 GILSTON ROAD LONDON SW10 9SR 01-373 7423

1/5/94

Dear Axel, on the Kitchen tree
there is not space for wet
dishes as one person is washing
them & piling them up. BZ 4372
Do you have a spare rack
on a ring that we
could attach lower
down the tree to drip into the
sink? Please?
Love Alison

Alison Smithson, [1 May 1994] circa 1984

1/5/94

Dear Axel, on the kitchen tree there is not space for wet dishes as one person is washing them & piling them up.
Do you have a spare rack that we [a sketch of a rack] could attach lower down the tree to drip into the sink? Please?
Love Alison

Wrongly dated (Alison died 14 August 1993). The Kitchen Tree is a free-standing minimum kitchen, based on an idea of Stefan Wewerka to complete his Cella living unit. It was designed collectively at Tecta in 1984, so the postcard might be from that year.

Alison Smithson, 21 May 1985

[Stamp] Singapore 21.5.85

Dear Axel, I started on the porch before I left but I find I need the exact dimensions of the doors: on your photograph they do not look equal.
Plan [a sketch of the doors, with question marks for the missing measurements along with the notes "measured when doors open" and "hinge side", plus a doodle asking about the shape of a certain part, offering two options]
I would like to know by the 2nd week of June when I will be back in London. I hope the interior & the pavilion are OK. AMS.

The doors referred to here are the "as-found" garden doors that were recycled for Axel's Porch, the first intervention by Alison Smithson at the Hexenhaus.

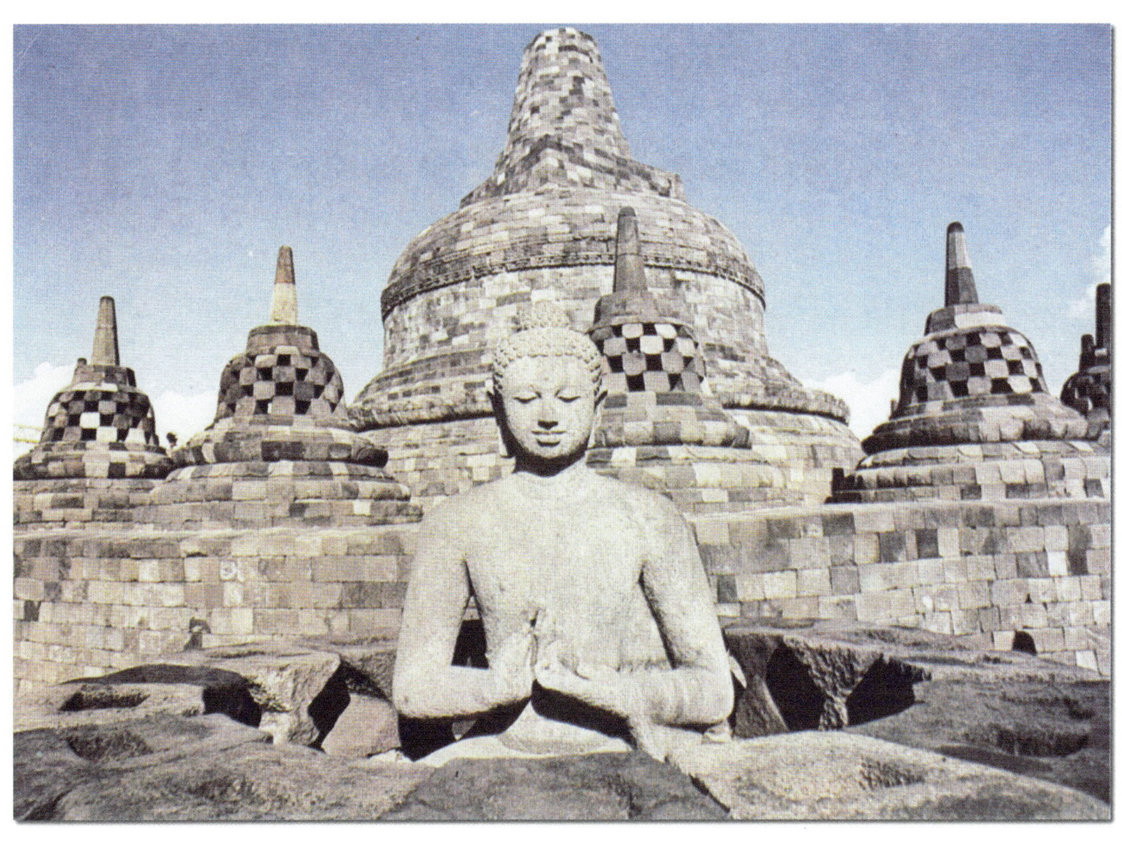

2.150 BARCELONA
Plaza de Toros "Monumental"
Place de Taureaux "Monumental"
Bullfighting arena "Monumental"
Stierkämpferzirkus "Monumental"

Alison Smithson, 17 November 1985

17/11/85

Dear Axel, Thank you for sending the catalogue to the people here who wanted to buy some/one of our furniture. I am here for the 3rd time this autumn with one more visit before Christmas and then in January & February: so I seem to be running "like Axel" all my days now.

Thank you for sending us the latest packet of photographs: we all like the two of me lecturing because they are so unusual a contrast: white hat and black background. Tell Karlchen they must have very big cats here because they have to build very big round baskets for them. Alison

The photos mentioned in the text were taken at the opening of the Tecta Pavilion, designed by Stefan Wewerka in 1985, where Alison delivered the inaugural lecture.

FESTINA
FESTINA
CAMPARI
ANIS Y RON PUJOL
METAL-MAZDA
Zerkowitz

Alison Smithson, 30 November 1985

Barcelona: 30/11/85

Dear Axel: Here again, still watching the Mies pavilion go up (perhaps I bring the slides in March for Stefan + Alexander to look at because some sort of comment might make the Mies look different) Peter is writing like crazy for your chair Museum: you will hear from him very soon. I hope Karlchen gets lots of cat food in his Christmas stocking.
Regards Alison.

Alison Smithson, 21 March 1986

Dear Axel,
Thank you for more 1930's and for sending your catalogue to Indonesia.
Would you like to send a catalogue? to Theo Crosby
    Pentagram Design Ltd
    11 Needham Road
    London W.11.
(was Oud the inventor of the grille on the wall for the 1920's?)
Alison.
[Notes in between, probably by Axel]:
1929
OUD
HOUSE AT WEISSENHOFF
INTERIOR

Alison refers to *The 1930's*, a book written by the Smithsons and published by Tecta and Alexander Verlag in 1985.
Theo Crosby was a good friend of Alison and Peter Smithson, and the technical editor (under Monica Pidgeon's editorship) of *Architectural Design* magazine, which regularly published texts by the Smithsons.

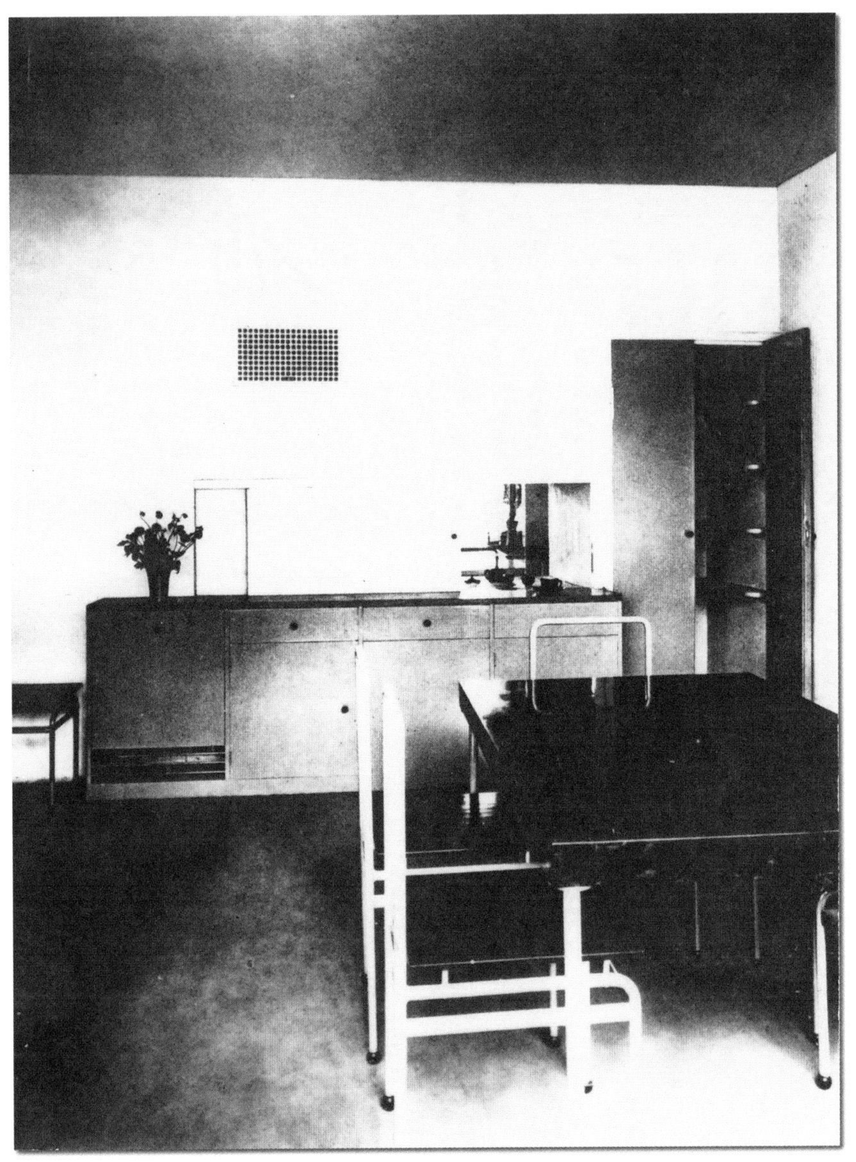

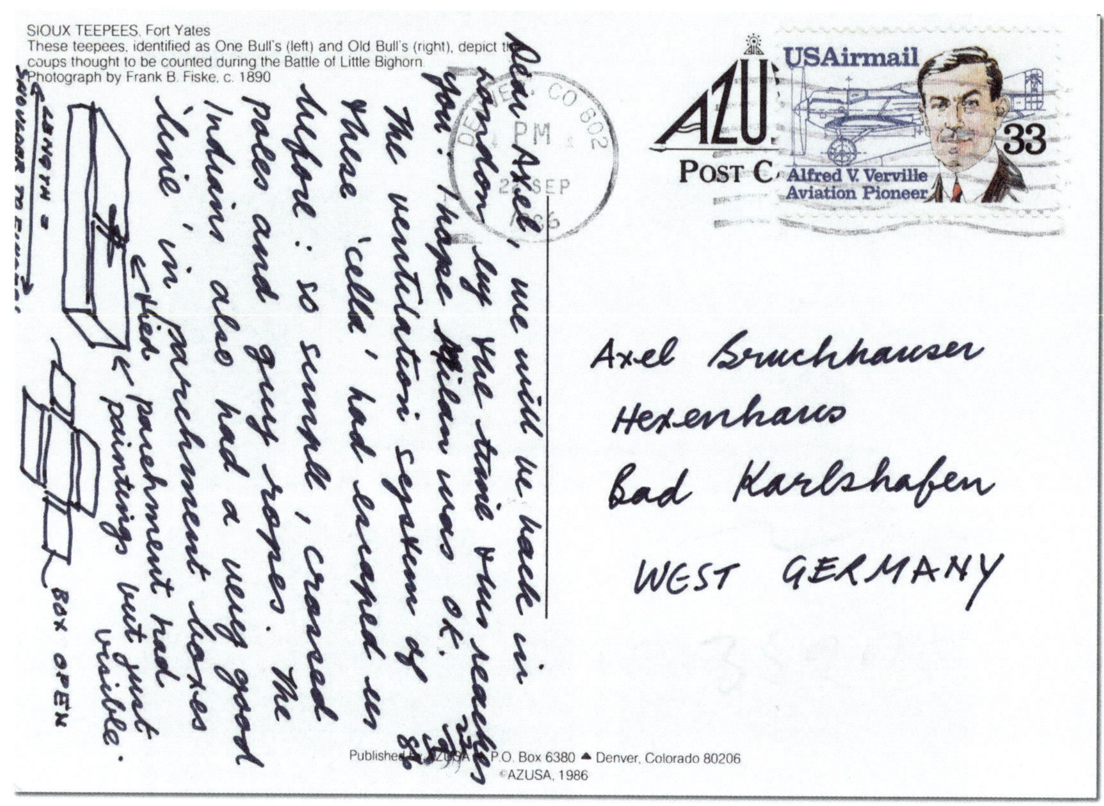

Alison Smithson, 22 September 1986

[Stamp] Denver 22 SEP 1986

Dear Axel, we will be back in London by the time this reaches you: I hope Milan was OK. The ventilation system of these 'cella' had escaped us before: so simple, crossed poles and guy ropes. The Indians also had a very good 'line' in parchment boxes
[drawings of an open box and a closed box, with notes]: tied; parchment had paintings but just
visible
BOX OPEN
LENGTH = SHOULDER TO…
[text cut off]

Unsigned.

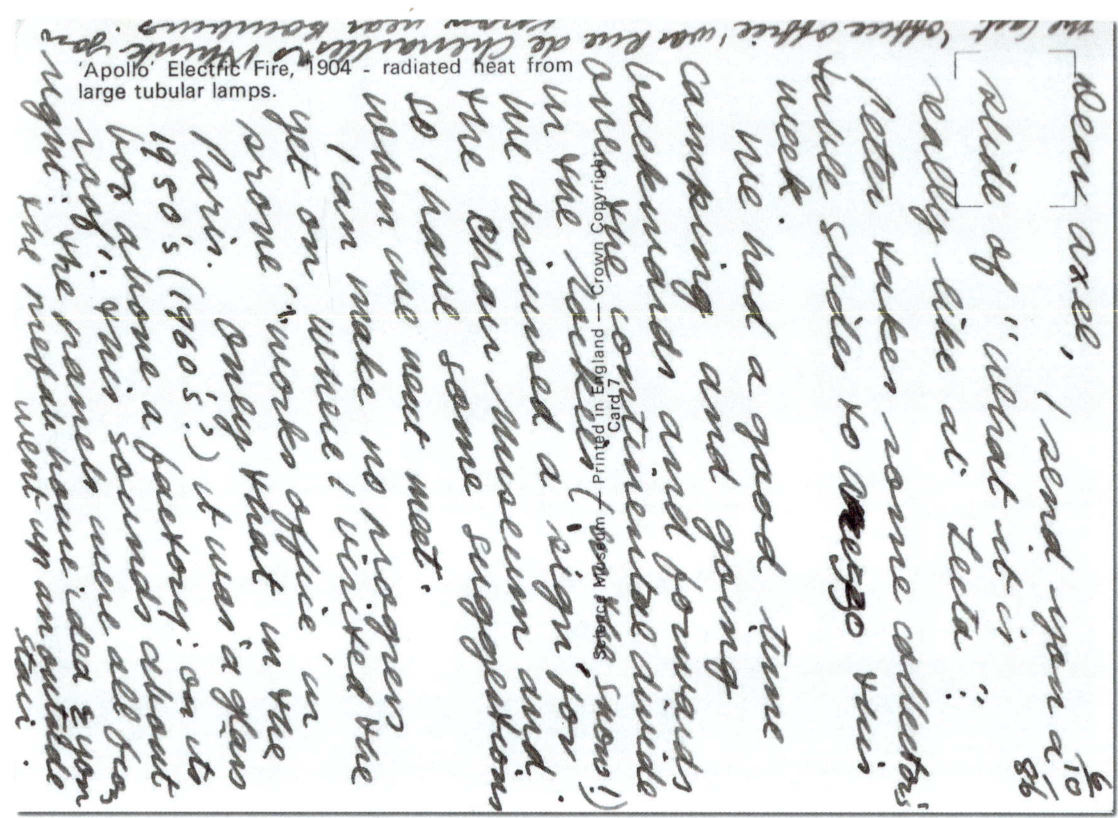

Alison Smithson, 6 October 1986

6/10/86

Dear Axel,
I send you a slide of "what it is really like at Tecta": Peter takes some collector's table slides to atrezzo this week.
We had a good time camping and going backwards and forwards over the continental divide in the Rockies (in the snow!). We discussed a 'sign' for the chair museum and so I have some suggestions when we next meet.
I can make no progress yet on where I visited the Prouvé 'works office' in Paris. Only that the 1950's (1960's?) it was a glass box above a factory: on its roof: This sounds about right: the panels were all from the prefab house idea & you went up an outside stair.

[text continues on the side]
The last 'office office' was Rue de Chenailles as I think you know near Bauhaus.

Unsigned.

THIMONNIER'S SEWING MACHINE
Replica of the first practical chainstitch machine invented in 1830.

Science Museum — Printed in England — Crown copyright
Card 49

Alison Smithson, 30 October 1986

30/10/86

Dear Axel,
We have had Mies drinking Karlchen's health 'round the clock' (in Düsseldorfs Uerige) so we hope he is now better. Herewith the two slides I took when we were with Heinz Rasch — for your records. It is dull and wet here but I think even if it is like this with you, your beech woods will be a very good colour to pass through every day. Alison

Karlchen has been Axel Bruchhäuser's cat since the 1970s. To date, there have been five generations of Karlchens.

MICHEL WAXMANN
Lettre du Sénégal

Alison Smithson, undated / circa 1986

[Comment on the postcard - in Peter Smithson's handwriting?]:
RENT-A-CHAIR: AFRIQUE

Dear Axel,
Werner Slager's letter was very vague but thank goodness it is Aachen: I look forward to going to that city again. Will you go to the symposium? I.e. should we fly into Hanover, speak about collector table (if it is ready in mock-up) & go by car together to Aachen? You decide what you want of us. The onyx has been found in a dis-used quarry in Algeria so now the last wall can be made in the pavilion. Best wishes
Alison

[note at the top of the postcard]:
(in Barcelona they say they are having a Mies lamp design made up that was never made before.

Postcard probably from 1986: a symposium for the centennial of Mies van der Rohe's birth was held in Aachen that year. Also, the reconstruction of the Barcelona pavilion was underway. "Onyx" refers to the rare auburn-red stone used for the reconstruction of the Mies van der Rohe Barcelona Pavilion in 1986.

TARÉDJI
TARÉDJI
TARÉDJI
TARÉDJI
TARÉDJI
TARÉDJI

Make-up table designed by Sheraton for Sarah Siddons, circa 1760.
From the British Theatre Museum, Leighton House, London, W.14.
COPYRIGHT Photograph by Houston Rogers.

Deutschland
Bucherbogen
Stadtbahnbogen 593 Am Savignyplatz
Berlin
Buchhandlung L. Werner
Residenzstrasse 18
München

Alison Smithson, undated / circa 1986

Dear Axel,
In *Quaderns* 171/1986 (Oct-Nov-December) there are 2 articles on Jean Prouvé with some pictures but with figures missing that must have been technical details (pages 39-51). Here are the German distributors [arrow pointing to address] of the magazine in case you want a copy for your collection. We have a student (from Geneva) who is drawing very good small axonometries of all our furniture in the hope they will be used in the Rome catalogue next year. We will show you also when they are finished.
Our Samantha now lives in Holland instead of Borneo so we may come to Europe more often.

Unsigned.

[Piece of paper stapled to the postcard]:
Deutschland
Bucherbogen
Stadtbahbogen 593 Am Savignyplaz
Berlin
Buchhandlung L. Werner
Residenzstrasse 18
München

[written on top with a pencil]: 030/3121932

Alison followed the professional press carefully, and in 1986 she was a visiting professor at ETSAB Barcelona. This postcard was probably written straight after the *Quaderns* magazine came out.

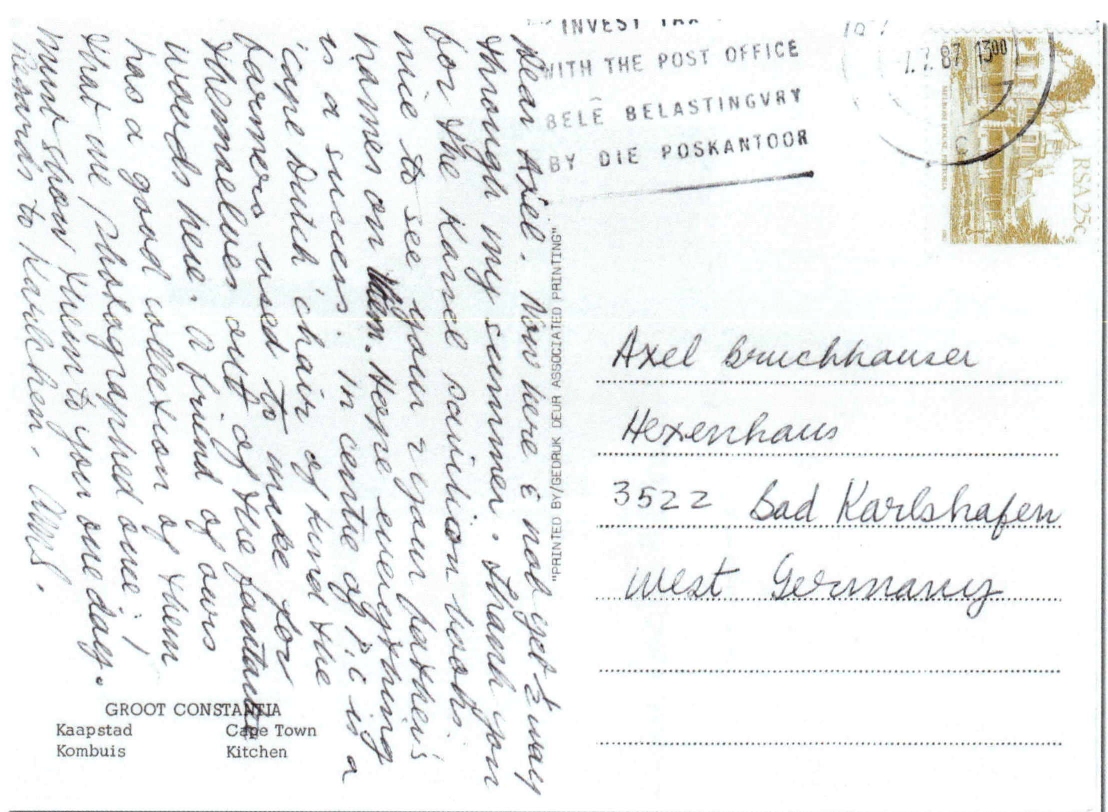

Alison Smithson, 7 July 1987

Dear Axel. Now here & not yet ½ way through my summer. Thank you for the Kassel pavilion books. Nice to see your and your father's names on them. Hope everything is a success. In centre of P.C [postcard] is a 'cape Dutch' chair of kind the farmers used to make for themselves out of the fantastic woods here. A friend of ours has a good collection of them that we photographed once: I must show them to you one day.
Regards to Karlchen. AMS.

Stefan Wewerka's design for the Tecta pavilion (1985) was replicated at the documenta 8 Art Fair in Kassel, 1987. It was then dismantled and rebuilt on the premises of the Kunstakademie Münster as an exhibition pavilion, and became known as the Wewerka pavilion.

Alison Smithson, 17 November 1987

17/11/87

Dear Axel, Thank you for the transparencies of the waterlily fish desk. Now I can show them in Holland. I like your November chair find. At Aram's Designer's Sat show Paolozzi showed his travelling artists drawers/chest/chair in its original old bits of wood and rope as well as a closed + open new wood, strap version that Aram's have: so, as I said, Aram is a clever fox. He thinks the new Eileen Gray book is too expensive at £40 and so does the publisher here but it was made in America.
[Written on the side]:
Love to good Karlchen.

Unsigned.

The British artist Eduardo Paolozzi was a founding member of the Independent Group and a close friend and collaborator of the Smithsons.
Aram is a gallery and design store in London, founded by Zeev Aram in 1964.

Kantoor en Fabrieksgebouwen van
De Erven de Wed. J. van Nelle N.V.
te Rotterdam

Copyright KLM AEROCARTO n.v. Den Haag nr. 2207

Photoprinted in the Netherlands

1070

Alison Smithson, undated / circa 1987

Dear Axel, I enclose the prompt reply from Ursula Goldfinger re Charlotte Perriand… in case you have a moment you cannot think what to do! If you need anything done in Holland: we have just had staying the girl who did all the photographic reproductive and layout work & saw AS in DS through the press at Delft (her English is excellent & Dutch people have many languages) WIENKE SCHELTENS, OOSTEINDE 41, 2611 UB DELFT. She still (4 yrs later) has lots of energy and is a nice person to work with & have around.

Unsigned.

The postcard could be from 1987, as the Smithsons were teaching at TU Delft in 1983-84 and Alison's book *AS in DS: An Eye on the Road* was published there in 1983, four years before the postcard.
Ursula Goldfinger (née Blackwell) was the widow of the Hungarian-born British architect and furniture designer Ernő Goldfinger. Charlotte Perriand worked with Goldfinger designing offices for the French railways.

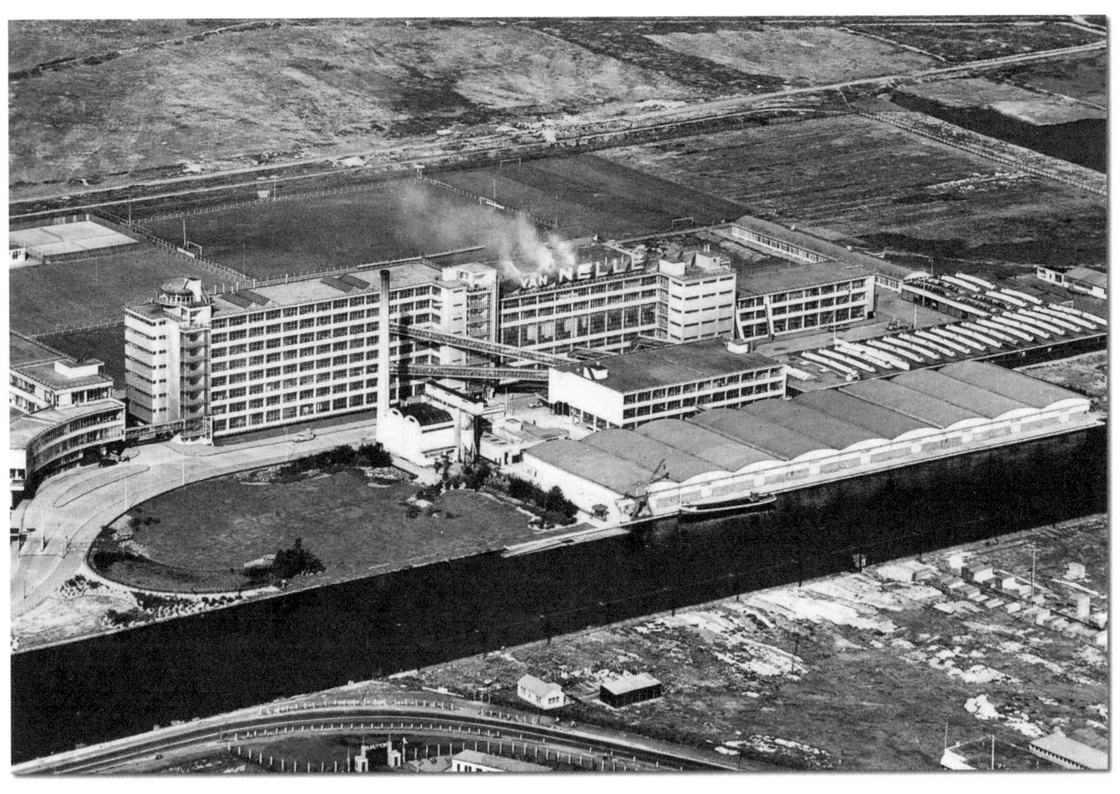
VAN NELLE

东宫门
East Palace Gate

中国旅游出版社 China Travel and Tourism Press

Dear Axel, Tell Karlchen that the cats are much bigger here and sit by very colourful porches. I am here for three weeks but Peter is at home if you want anything. I hope all goes well for Kassel. Best wishes for success.
Alison M Smithson

台湾民居
90分 中国人民邮政

AXEL BRUCHHAUSER
HEXENHAUS
3522 BAD KARSHAFEN
WEST GERMANY

Alison Smithson, undated / circa 1987

Dear Axel, Tell Karlchen that the cats are much bigger here and sit by very colourful porches. I am here for three weeks but Peter is at home if you want anything. I hope all goes well for Kassel. Best wishes for success.
Alison M Smithson

Alison travelled to China in 1987, so the postcard is likely to be from that trip. She used to sign as AMS (Alison Margaret Smithson) in the early years.

Alison Smithson, undated / circa 1987

[surrounded with a line and with a note, plus doodles]:

Dear Axel, It was good to talk to you: it seemed both a natural connection and a magical continuation because I had spent the day working on the Cornell boxes with an actual set of graphics so as to test the box shapes.
As I said, we need to work on the ladders next and then return to fit boxes and ladders together: [a sketch of a structure leaning against the wall, with a 20° angle marked in the top joint] possibly starting with this idea?
Therefore the 'box' needing to be made in mock-up is Strewelpeter because it is an object and will have to have its own 'goal-posts' ladder to hold it high over another feature like an old fireplace, in a room [a sketch of a structure leaning on the wool and ground over a fireplace with a note]: or bracing to suit Strewelpeter
I like the sponge finish

The carpets are in their colour test stage but need another input which is why I asked about Jen: otherwise Martina was good to work with for Aedes Gallery (and may be the person behind Stefan's regrets because she is very sane).

23rd February 1988
to
12th March 1988
Monday – Saturday 11am – 7pm

YU-CHEE CHONG
2 Whitehorse Street, Mayfair, London W1Y 7LA
Telephone: 01-491 3826

FOLDER DESIGN BY OLIVER COLLIGNON

Furniture Designs
1830 - 1930

P.S Returns from Siena August 14 and apart from September 29 week to October 9. I could arrange perhaps to come over, if needed, before October 9. I have the sketches all together so no more preparation is needed before a visit. I will telephone nearer October 9 if we are not in touch before. Meanwhile Karlchen could be thinking why chairs made of wood do not have tails.
Love to you both,
Alison.

In 1986, Alison designed a wall cabinet inspired by Struwwelpeter's frazzled, pointy hair (Struwwelpeter, or "Shaggy Peter", was the unkempt title character of a children's story collection, written and illustrated by Heinrich Hoffmann in 1845). The prototype cabinet is at the Hexenhaus. The Cornell Boxes were designed in 1987-88. Since Alison mentions both of these designs, this might indicate that the postcard is from 1987.

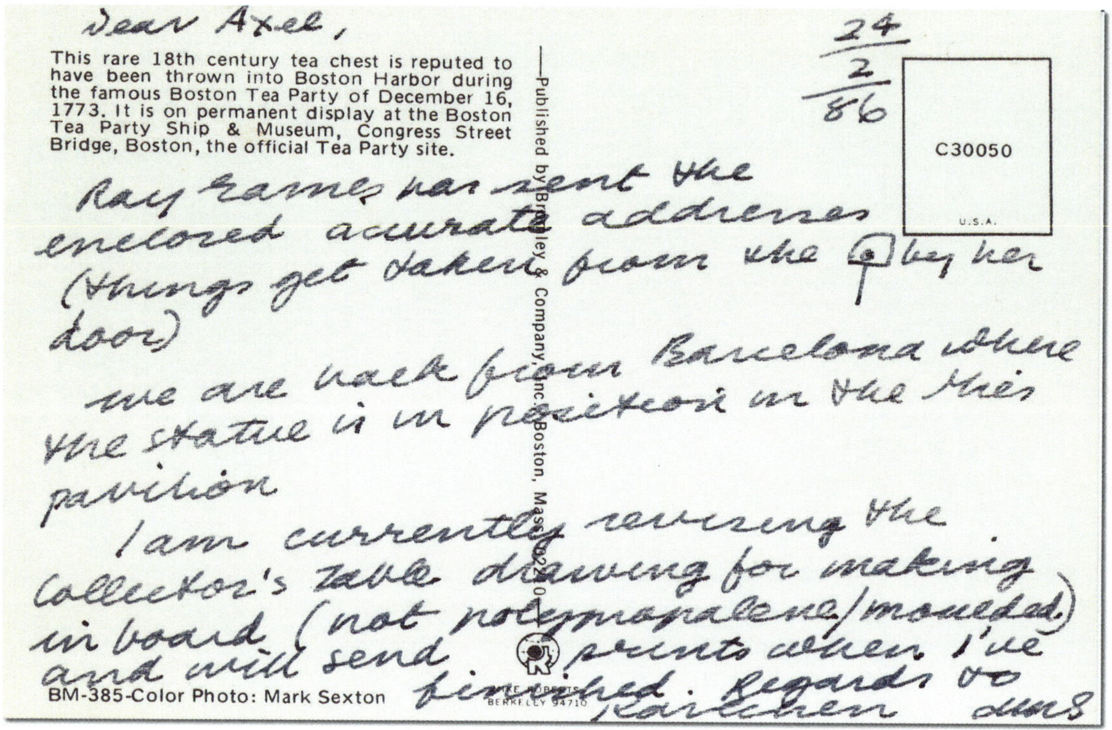
Dear Axel,

24
2
86

This rare 18th century tea chest is reputed to have been thrown into Boston Harbor during the famous Boston Tea Party of December 16, 1773. It is on permanent display at the Boston Tea Party Ship & Museum, Congress Street Bridge, Boston, the official Tea Party site.

Published by Bradley & Company, Inc. Boston, Mass.

C30050

U.S.A.

Ray Eames has sent the enclosed accurate addresses (things get taken from the [doodle] by her door)

we are back from Barcelona where the statue is in position in the Mies pavilion

I am currently revising the collector's table drawing for making in board (not polypropylene/moulded) and will send prints when I've finished. Regards to Karlchen AMS

BM-385-Color Photo: Mark Sexton

Alison Smithson, 24 February 1988

24/2/86

Dear Axel,
Ray Eames has sent the enclosed accurate addresses (things get taken from the "skip" by her door) [i.e. doodle of a person skipping]
We are back from Barcelona where the statue is in position in the Mies pavilion.
I am currently revising the collector's table drawing for making in board (not polypropylene/moulded) and will send prints when I've finished. Regards to Karlchen
AMS

Georg Kolbe's statue *Dawn* (initially wrongly referred to as *The Dancer*) is located in the small pond of the reconstructed Barcelona Pavilion by Mies van der Rohe.
The Collector's Table was designed by Alison in 1986, and was featured in the Tecta catalogue in 1987 and 1992. The final design was made out of lacquered plywood board with textile and plexiglass details.

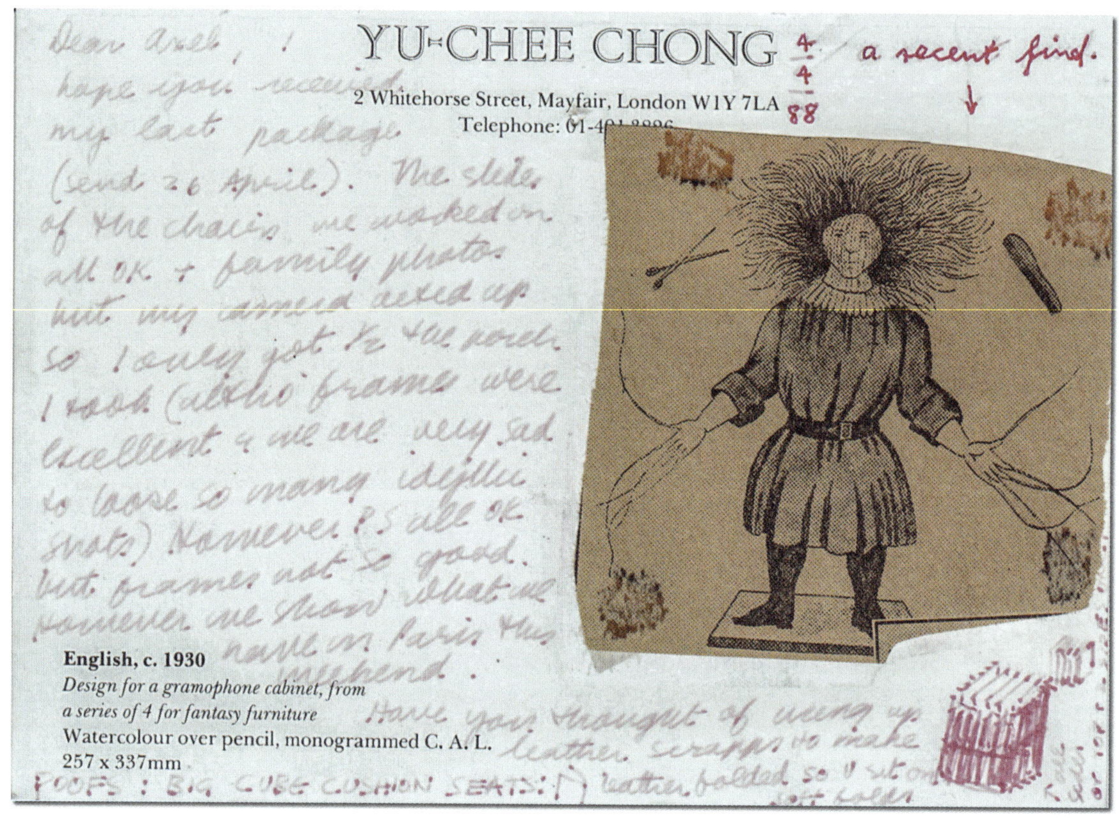

Alison Smithson, 4 April 1988

4/4/88

Dear Axel, I hope you received my last package (send 26 April). The slides of the chairs we worked on all OK + family photos but my camera acted up so I only got ½ the porch I took (all the frames were excellent & we are very sad to loose so many idyllic shots). However PS all OK but frames not so good. However we show what we have in Paris this weekend. Have you thought of using up leather scrapps to make POOFS: BIG CUBE CUSHION SEATS: [a tiny sketch of a fold] leather folded so u sit on soft folds [a doodle of a pouffe with folds, and a text pointing to the drawing:] all sides or TOP + B SIDES [illegible].

[glued onto the postcard: a newspaper clipping of an illustration of Struwwelpeter, with a comment]: a recent find

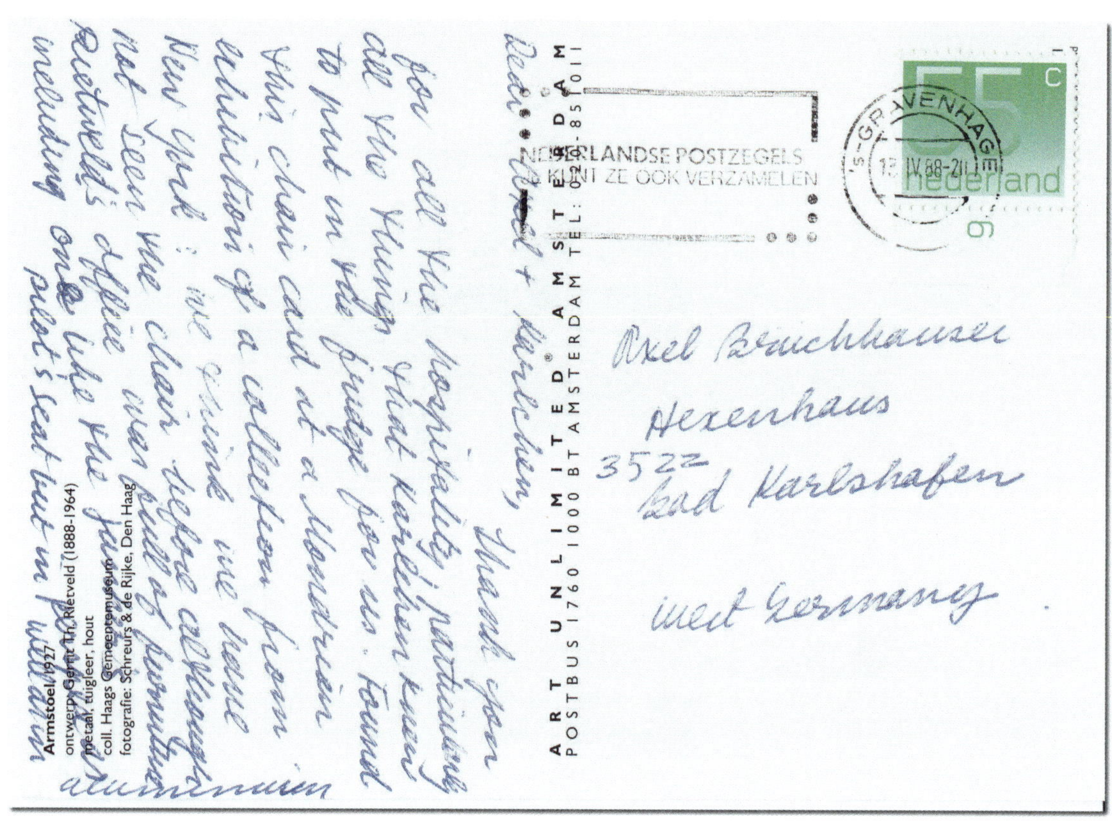

nederland 55 c
'S-GRAVENHAGE 13 IV 88
NEDERLANDSE POSTZEGELS
JE KUNT ZE OOK VERZAMELEN
ART UNLIMITED® AMSTERDAM
POSTBUS 1760 1000 BT AMSTERDAM TEL: 020-851011
Axel Bruchhauser
Hexenhaus
3522
Bad Karlshafen
West Germany
Armstoel, 1927
ontwerp: Gerrit Th. Rietveld (1888-1964)
metaal, tuigleer, hout
coll. Haags Gemeentemuseum
fotografie: Schreurs & de Rijke, Den Haag

Alison Smithson, 14 April 1988

Dear Axel + Karlchen,
Thank you for all the hospitality, particularly all the things that Karlchen knew to put in the fridge for us. Found this chair card at a Mondrian exhibition of a collector from New York: we think we have not seen the chair before although Rietweld's office was full of furniture including one like the Junker's pilot's seat but in perspex as well as in aluminium.

Unsigned.

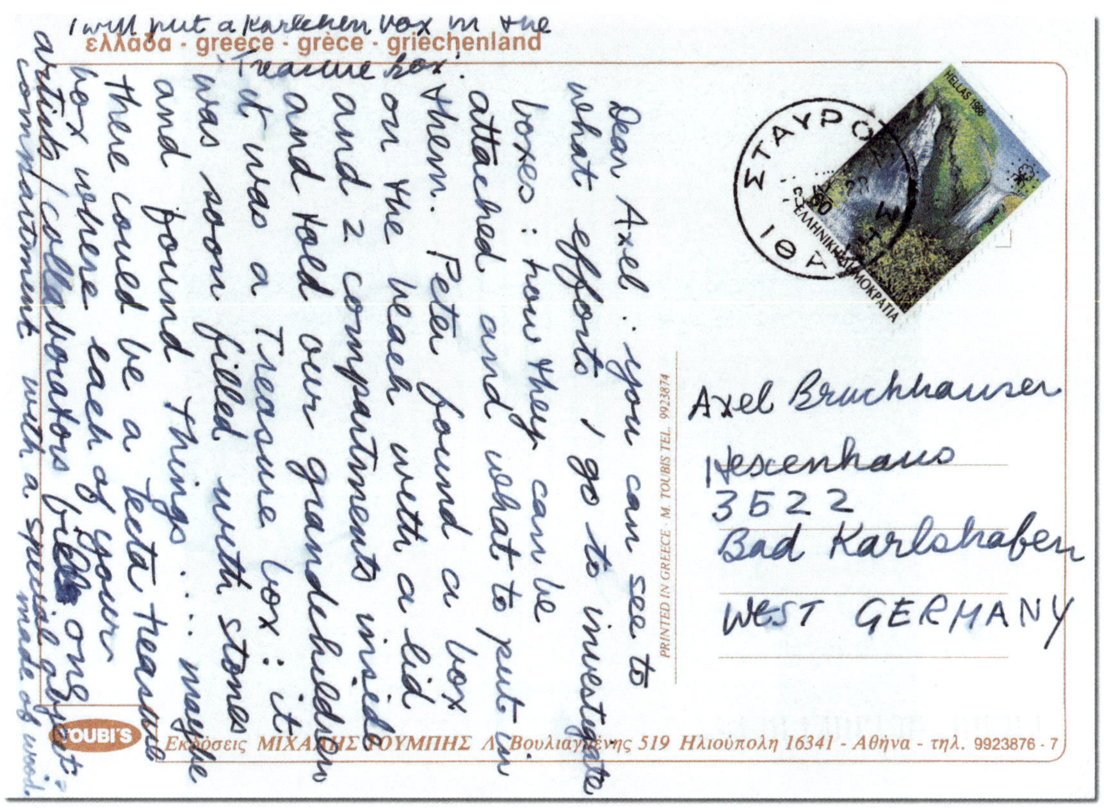

Alison Smithson, 8 September 1988

Dear Axel: You can see to what effort I go to investigate boxes: how they can be attached and what to put in them. Peter found a box on the beach with a lid and 2 compartments inside and told our grandchildren it was a Treasure box: it was soon filled with stones and found things… maybe there could be a Tecta treasure box where each of your artists / collaborators fill one compartment with a special object: made of wood.
[Written on the side]:
I will put a Karlchen box in the 'Treasure Box'.

Unsigned.

Alison designed different box furniture pieces for Tecta; the Economist Red Box set (1984), the Cornell Boxes (1987-88) and the Collector's Table (1987) with box-like containers.

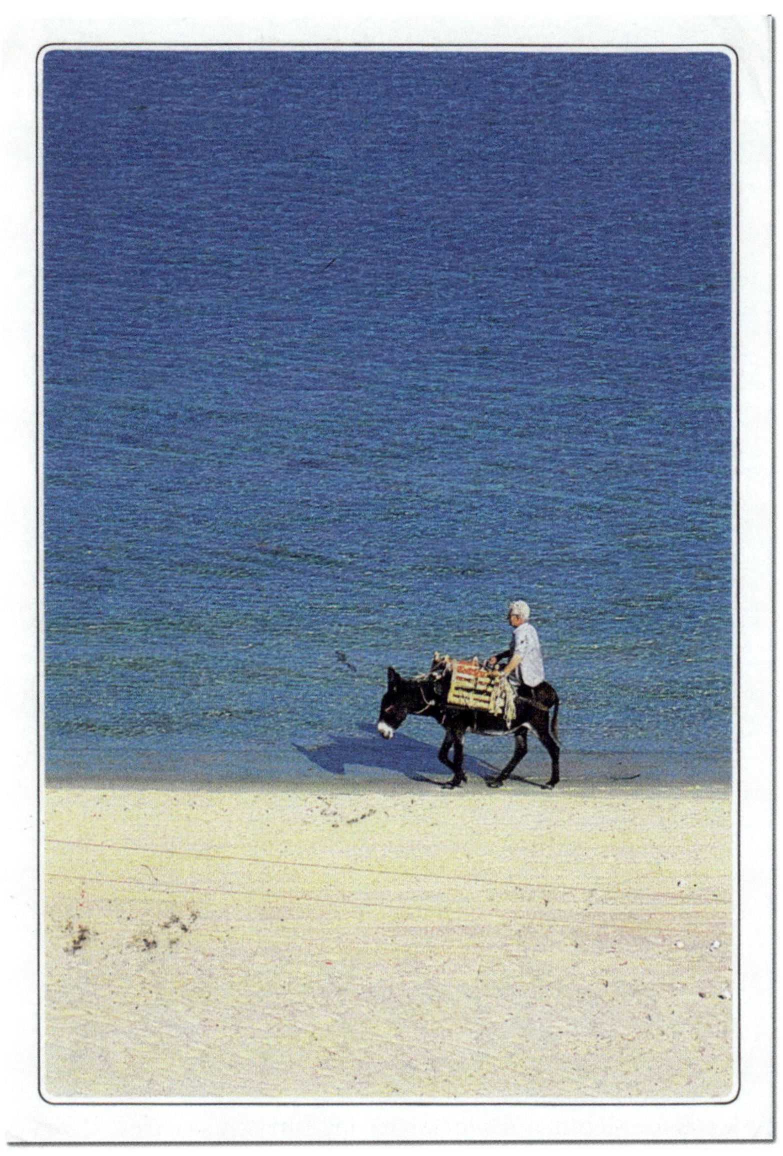

Kungliga Tekniska Högskolan räknar sina anor tillbaka till det *Laboratorium mechanicum* som Christopher Polhem grundade 1697. Det var en teknisk läroanstalt som skulle ge eleverna en grundlig utbildning i mekanik.

1700-talets maskiner var nästan helt byggda i trä och det var därför naturligt att i första hand instruera eleverna i hur trä kunde användas som konstruktionsmaterial i maskintekniken. Som hjälpmedel i undervisningen lät Polhem konstruera ett "mekaniskt alfabet", en serie trämodeller som visade alla dåtidens maskinelement. Han ansåg att "Lika nödvändigt som det är för en boksynt att prompt ha i minnet alla de ord av vilka en mening är sammansatt, lika nödvändigt är det för en *mekanikus* att ha i sinnet alla de enkla delar varav en maskin är sammansatt". På bilden syns en av "bokstäverna".

Modellsamlingens vidare öden följde utvecklingen av det svenska tekniska undervisningsväsendet och flyttades först till Kungl. Modellkammaren, sedan till Mekaniska Skolan och slutligen till Teknologiska Institutet (numera Kungl Tekniska Högskolan). På 1920-talet återfanns samlingen på vinden till Tekniska Högskolans gamla byggnader på Drottninggatan och idag finns den utställd på Tekniska Museet.

25/11/88

The Royal Institute of Technology originated from the Laboratorium Mechanicum which Christopher Polhem started in 1697. It was a technical training organization providing students with a basic education in mechanics.

The 18th century machines were almost entirely built of wood and so the students were trained primarily to use wood wherever possible. To assist in the training Polhem designed a 'Mechanical Alphabet', a series of wooden models representing all of the machine elements existing at that time. He maintained that "Just as an author should have in mind all the words needed to construct a sentence, so a mechanical engineer should have in sight all the elements needed to construct a machine". The picture shows one of these 'Building Blocks'.

The 'Mechanical Alphabet' followed the technical school location and moved first to the Royal Model Chamber, then to the School of Mechanics and finally to the Technological Institute, now called the Royal Institute of Technology. Around 1920 the collection was re-discovered in the attic of the schools old building on Drottninggatan. Today it is exhibited at the Technical Museum in Stockholm.

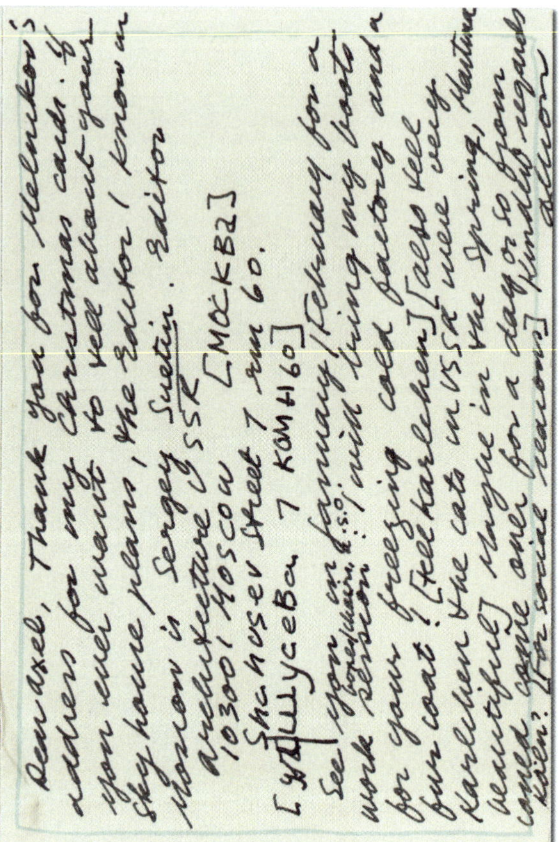

Alison Smithson, 25 November 1988

25/11/88

Dear Axel, Thank you for Melnikov's address for my Christmas cards. If you ever want to tell about your sky house plans, the editor I know in Moscow is Sergey Suetin.

Editor Architecture USSR
103001 MOSCOW [*Москва*]
Schahusev Street 1 km60.
[*Шущусева* 1 KOM H 60]

See you in January / February for a work session [written above]: boxes/chairs a.s.o. [and so on] I will bring my boots for your freezing cold factory and a fur coat! [tell Karlchen] [also tell Karlchen the cats in USSR were very beautiful] Maybe in the spring, Martina could come over for a day or so from Köln? [For social reasons]
Kindest regards
Alison

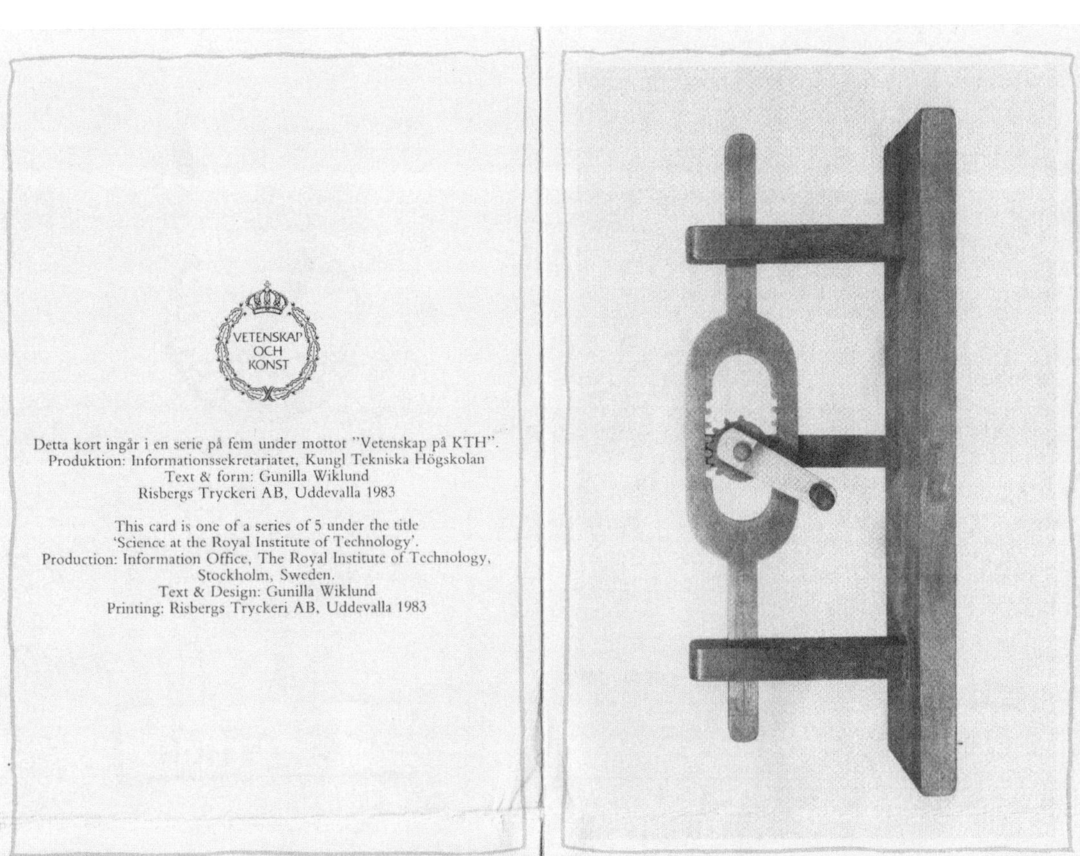
VETENSKAP
OCH
KONST
Detta kort ingår i en serie på fem under mottot "Vetenskap på KTH".
Produktion: Informationssekretariatet, Kungl Tekniska Högskolan
Text & form: Gunilla Wiklund
Risbergs Tryckeri AB, Uddevalla 1983
This card is one of a series of 5 under the title
'Science at the Royal Institute of Technology'.
Production: Information Office, The Royal Institute of Technology,
Stockholm, Sweden.
Text & Design: Gunilla Wiklund
Printing: Risbergs Tryckeri AB, Uddevalla 1983

Alison Smithson, undated / circa 1988

Dear Axel, I hope Milan went OK. I flew into Samarkand this morning. The weather beautiful. Hope to see you within the next two months to work with you on some of the box ideas, and so on. Karlchen will be glad you are back from 'mousing' in Milan. Love Alison.

The postcard must be from October 1988, as Alison visited the city of Samarkand (then USSR, now Uzbekistan) that year.

Alison Smithson, 1 February 1989

Zurich: 1/2/89

Dear Axel, At present the other side of the mountains from you. Thank you very much for the Christmas plate: it looks very good on top of our red box. I hope the [drawing of a Tecta tube aplati symbol] chair sells well. We still think the top has to 'come into line' with the idea of nipping the tube 'identify' the difference.
[written vertically to the side] Love to Karlchen
Alison.

Tecta developed and patented the Jean Prouvé-inspired solution of a flattened tube, the tube aplati, in order to strengthen the tubular cantilever chair legs at the curves. The solution gave place to a graphic sign illustrating the transformation of the tube.

B
MILITÄR
FLUGKONKURRENZ
DÜBENDORF
11. und 12. OKTOBER
bei Nichtflugwetter 18. und 19. ev. 25. und 26. OKt.
GEBR. FRETZ A.G. ZÜRICH

Alison Smithson, 22 April 1989

Edinburgh. 22·4·89

Dear Axel, Thank you for new catalogues. Can you please remember that when you next have photographs taken of furniture in an all white 'studio' setting that I would still like to have the waterlily/fish desk fully documented: ① the frame; ② frame + 'waterlilies'; ③ frame + surface + waterlilies; ④ frame + surface + waterlilies + boxes ⑤ boxes + pedals in a 2nd position. All in black + white so that it can be published. I could also do with 'studio' portraits in black & white of the collector's table. In ② positions (or ② views) please. We should try to fix a September / October work week.
[written vertically to the side] Love Alison

The Waterlily and Fish Desk and the Collector's Table were two experimental furniture designs that Tecta produced for some time. The Waterlily and Fish Desk is depicted in the postcards from 26 August 1992; 20 June 1992; 20 January 1993 and 24 March 1993, printed for the Smithsons' b.d exhibition in Madrid in 1992. The photos of these two tables were taken in 1989 by Tecta.

ST JOHN'S HEAD
painted and gilded alabaster in original painted oak frame
English (Nottingham), 15th century
40 x 24cm (16¾ x 10in)
The Burrell Collection
Reg no 1/34
©Glasgow Museums & Art Galleries

Alison Smithson, 12 October 1989

[written on front of postcard]
↑ I like the Sauna.

12/10/89

Dear Axel, Thinking more about November I think I should travel Leiden → Lauenforde Saturday November 11th on the Amsterdam 10:59 train arriving Lauenforde 17:16 (so we get Saturday evening Sunday discussion 3 workshop days) and return to Leiden on Thursday 16th
I hope this is OK.
I will telephone to confirm when I have the train tickets in Leiden on 10th November (because train times sometimes change in October here). An advance payment of 500 DM would be welcome and I will bring tickets to compare the totals.
Alison

Dear Axel
Here is your
'Turn of the Year' present.
I hope you & Karlchen
have a good 1990.
AMS.

(Sorry Karlchen, not a fish
in the pool)

ST JOHN'S HEAD
painted and gilded alabaster in original painted oak frame
English (Nottingham), 15th century
40 x 24cm (16¾ x 10in)
The Burrell Collection Reg no 1/34
©Glasgow Museums & Art Galleries

Alison Smithson, undated; late 1989/early 1990

Dear Axel
Here is your 'Turn of the Year' present. I hope you & Karlchen have a good 1990.
AMS.

(Sorry Karlchen, not a fish in the pool)

Unsigned.

The postcard seems to be a new year's greeting from the end of 1989.

Alison Smithson, undated / circa 1990

Dear Axel,
Thank you for the cheque. I will do the
canteen door
toilet windows
tiling as soon as I can in February.
There is a Rodchenko Stepanova exhibition here with an interesting red / black chess table and facing chairs + the 1925 Paris 'library' table / chairs + theatre sets: all reconstructions of course.

Unsigned.

The Tecta Canteen Porch and toilets, designed by Alison Smithson, were completed in 1990. The postcard could be from that year.

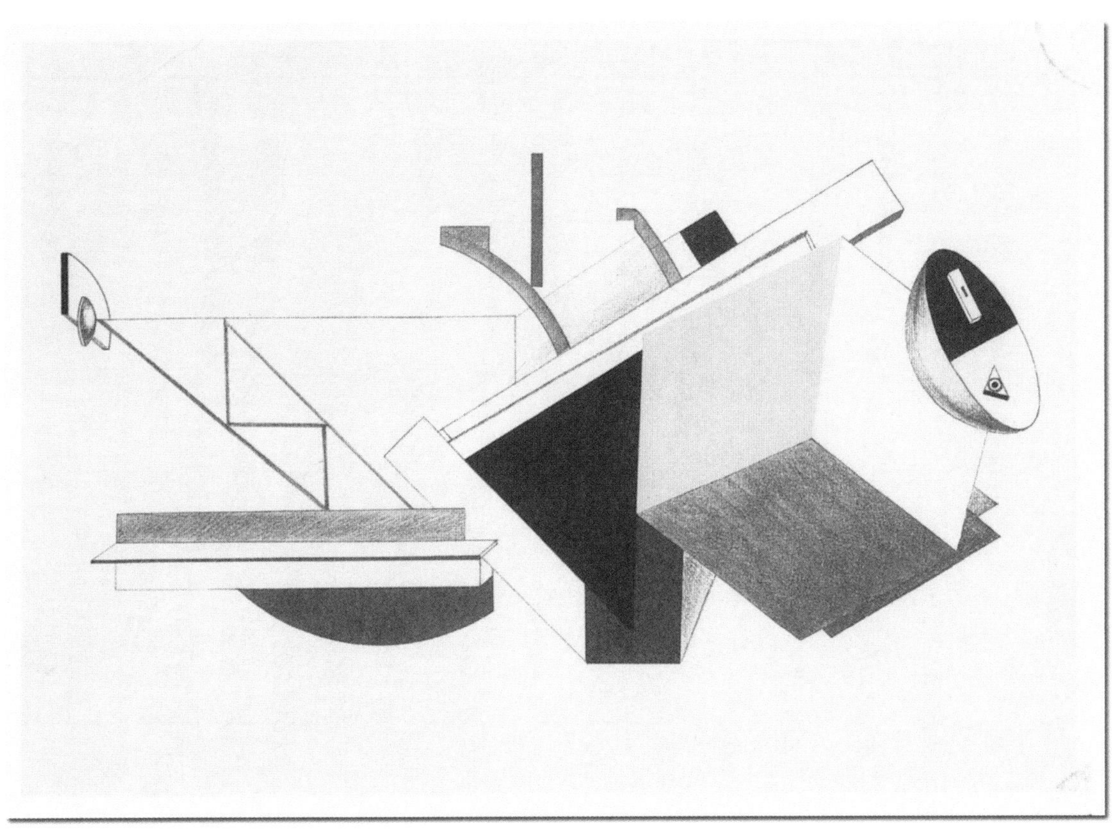

Dear Axel,
Can you get me engineer Pologni's home address please because our Christmas card to his brother Charles in Hungary was returned marked 'parti'.: which is odd as we have had no change of address & I should like to write to ask what has happened?
I look forward to looking out of the riverbank window & dreaming up fish for Karlchen.
5/1/90

El Lissitzky / victoire sur le soleil / Sieg über die Sonne / victory over the sun / vittoria sul sole / projet de marionnette mécanique pour l'Opéra futuriste de Krutschonykh / Ansager / l'annonceur / the announcer / l'annunciatore / lithographie 1923
© NOUVELLES IMAGES SA. éditeurs et Kunsthalle Bielefeld 1987 / CP 906 / offset printed in France

Alison Smithson, 5 January 1990

Dear Axel,
Can you get me engineer Pologni's home address please because our Christmas card to his brother Charles in Hungary was returned marked 'parti'... which is odd as we have had no change of address & I should like to write to ask what has happened?
I look forward to looking out of the riverbank window & dreaming up fish for Karlchen.

5/1/90

Unsigned.

The Hungarian architect Charles Pologni (Károly Polónyi) (1928-2002) was part of Team 10's wider circle.
Alison's third intervention on the Hexenhaus, the Riverbank window, was under construction during 1990. It is a bay window with a seat for both Axel and Karlchen, overlooking the River Weser.

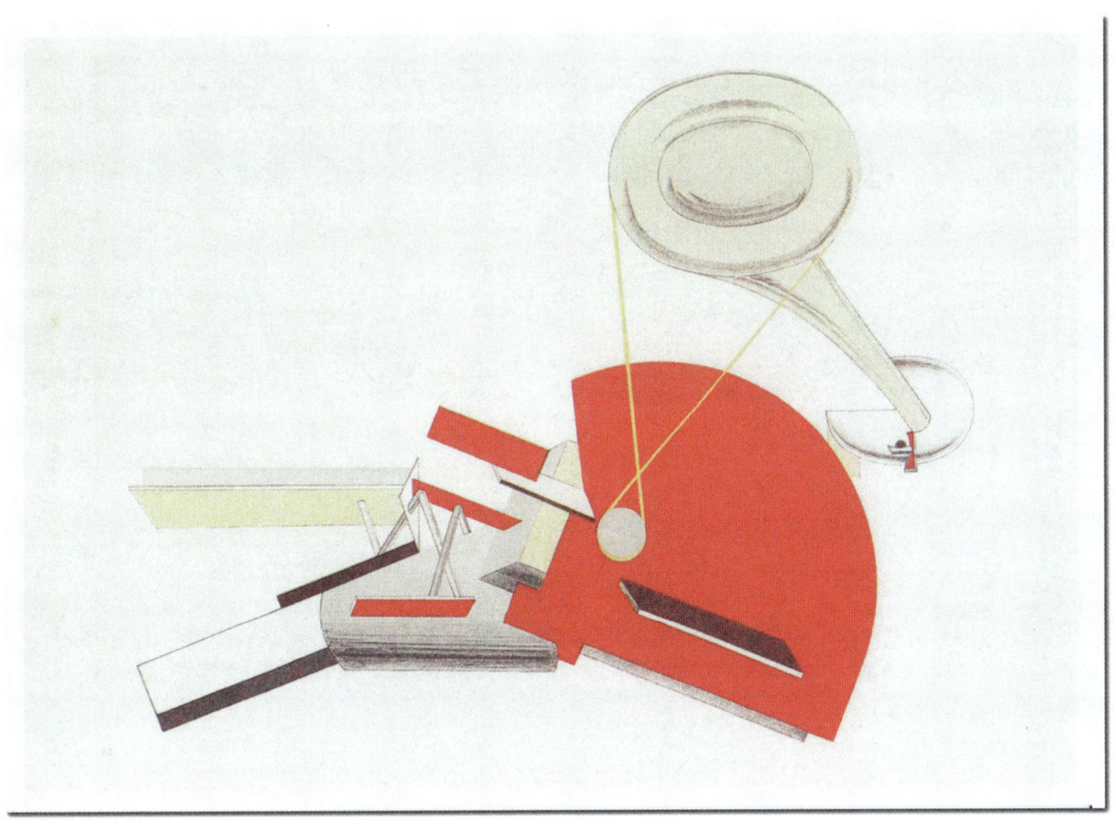

Alison Smithson, 11 February 1990

Dear Axel, We spent time in Berlin with Julius Posener – whose little book published by Ernst & Sohn I gave you (pictures of his childhood etc.). He is 85 so knew many architects of 1929… →. He was interested to hear of your Beverungen: can you please send him a Kragsthul?

PROFESSOR
JULIUS POSENER
BERLIN 37
KLIST STRASSE 21
ZELLENDORF

He is about to publish a book on Poelzig & his own full bibliography. He is still very active & his memory / knowledge are wonderful. We visited Potsdam where there is much Schinkel cast iron seats / benches / tables. Most in a blue grey matt colour. But we also like the dark green. Have you thought Schinkel in dark green: or dark green back & seat + white sides? Or white seat?

11/2/90

Unsigned.

Tecta still produces black cast-iron garden chairs and benches, as designed by Karl Friedrich Schinkel in the nineteenth century. Originally, they were produced at the state-owned Royal Prussian Iron Foundry in Berlin.

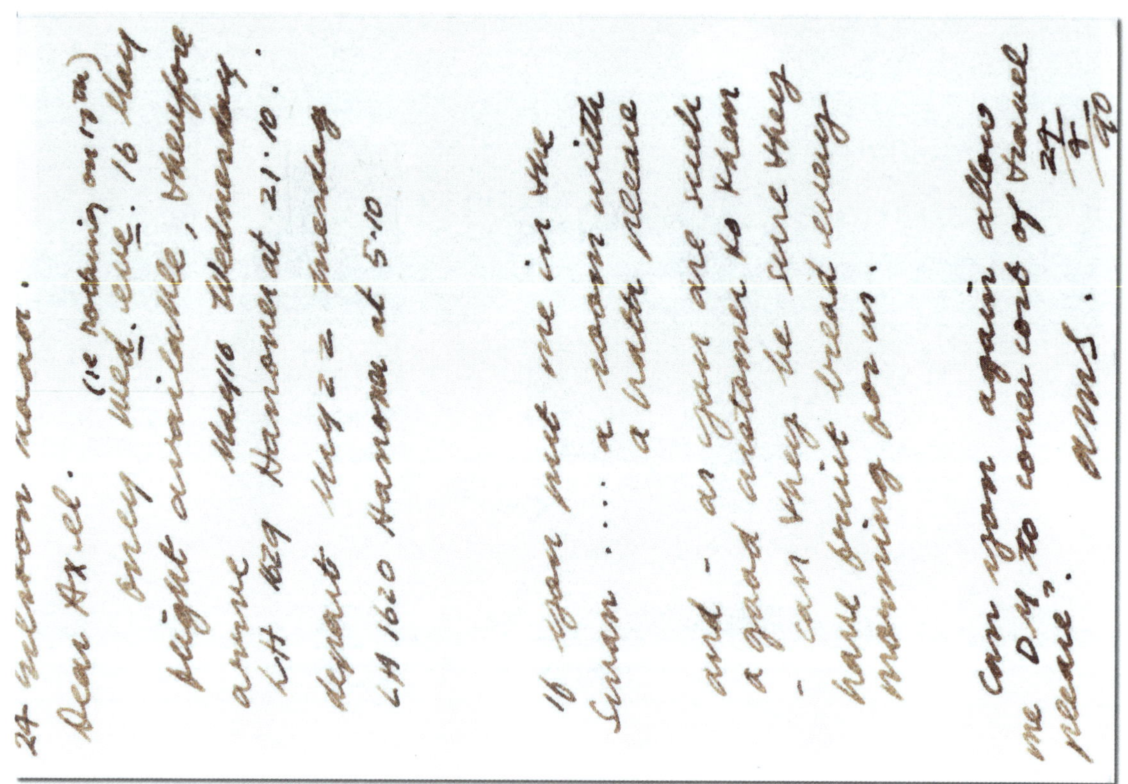

Alison Smithson, 24 April 1990

24 Gilston Road.
Dear Axel.
Only Wed. eve. 16 May (ie nothing on 17th) flight available, therefore arrive May 16 Wednesday LH 1629 Hanover at 21.10. Depart May 22 Tuesday LH 1620 Hanover at 5.10

If you put me in the Swan... a room with a bath please
and — as you are such a good customer to them — can they be sure they have fruit bread every morning for us.

Can you again allow me DM to cover cost of travel please?
AMS
24/4/90

When visiting Axel in Bad Karlshafen, Alison and Peter usually stayed at the traditional Hotel Zum Schwan.

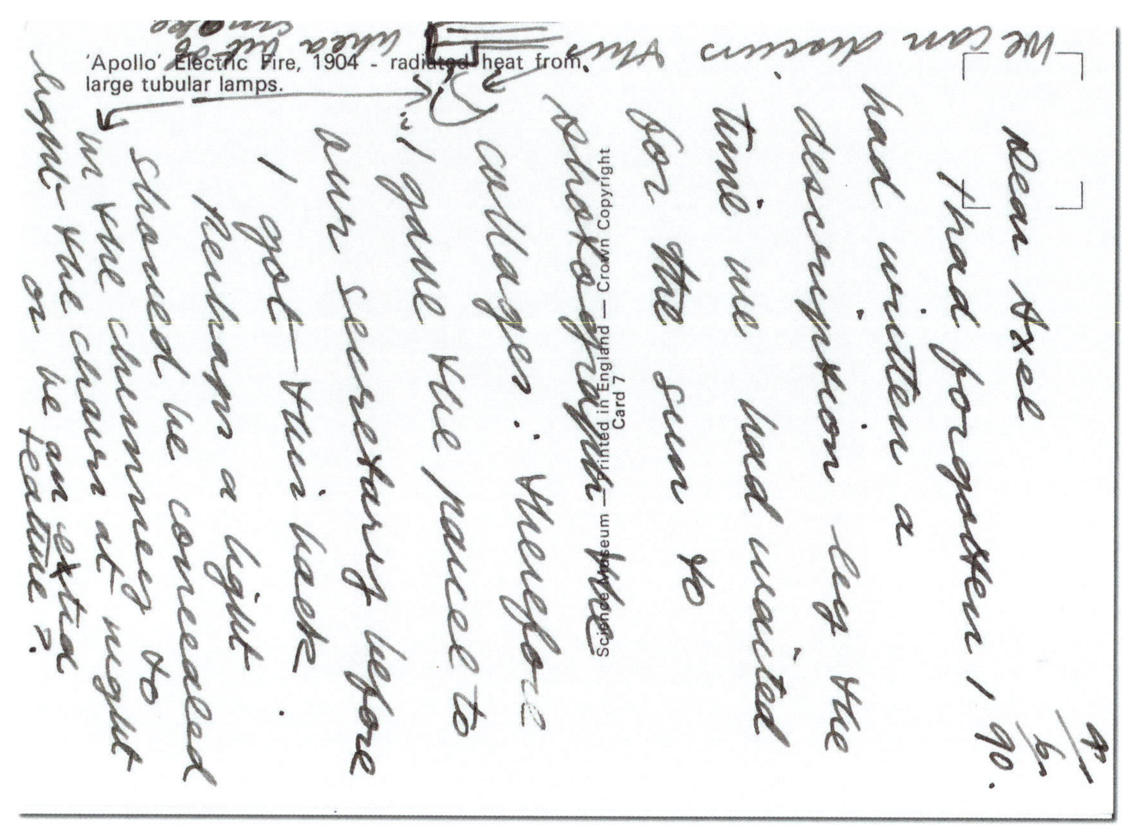

Alison Smithson, 4 June 1990

4/6/90

Dear Axel
I had forgotten I had written a description by the time we had waited for the sun to photograph the collages: therefore I gave the parcel to our secretary before I got this back. Perhaps a light should be concealed in the chimney to light the chairs at night or be an extra feature?
[Note at the side] We can discuss this [arrow to a sketch of a candle, and another arrow pointing at the previous sentence, with a question mark] like a bit of smoke

Unsigned.

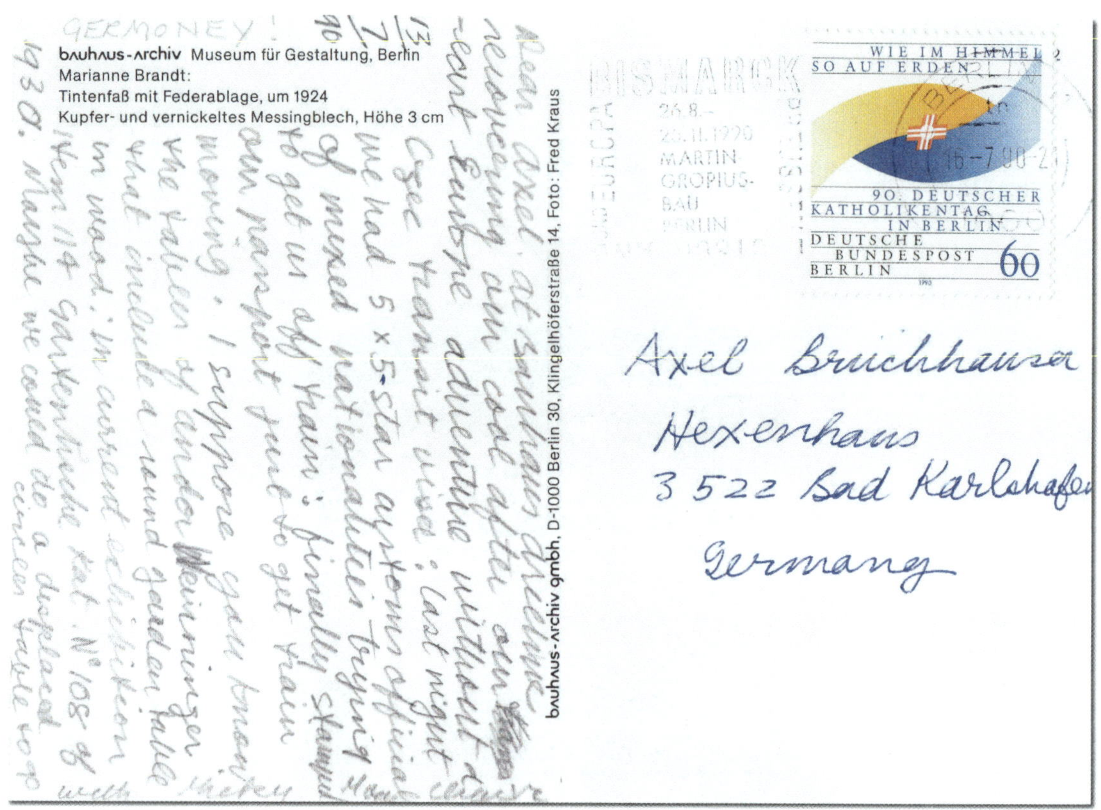

Alison Smithson, 13 July 1990

[Written above postcard details] GERMONEY!

[Stamp] Berlin 16.7.90

13/7/90

Dear Axel, at Bauhaus archive recovering our cool after our East Europe adventure without a Czec transit visa: last night we had 5 × 5-star customs officials of mixed nationalities trying to get us off train: finally stamped our passport just to get train moving. I suppose you know the tables of Andor Weininger that include a round garden table in wood: in current exhibition Item 114 Gartentische Kat. N° 108 of 1930. Maybe we could do a displaced circles table to go [text turns vertically] with Mickey Mouse chairs.

Unsigned.

Andor Weininger (1899–1986) was an architect, artist and designer born in Hungary. He trained at the Bauhaus and eventually emigrated to the United States. His round table designs are from 1922–49.

YU-CHEE CHONG [CHINESE FOR 'BAD TASTE IN FURNITURE']
2 Whitehorse Street, Mayfair, London W1Y 7LA
Telephone: 01-491 3826

Austrian, c. 1890
Project for a chamber organ
Pen and ink and watercolour, signed indistinctly lower right
380 x 552mm

Alison Smithson, 1 November 1990

[Next to Yu-Chee-Chong, i.e the name of a gallery, are a few words written in different handwriting – Peter's? – and in a different colour]:
[CHINESE FOR 'BAD TASTE IN FURNITURE']

1/11/90

Dear Axel,
I said I would hold Jerome's bills until Printer had set text. 'Mendle' (?) rang me and said you would have text by end of week. I can correct the English if you send it and then we simply await the time to do the layout. Not mid-November please: maybe the early December we said in Paris. To suit Karlchen. What is the Japanese cloth situation? Will you still try to upholster TT1 for the Fairs or have plans moved away from this idea? Thank you for the Paris lunch. AMS

Alison writes about the editing process of her book *Saint Jerome; The Desert…The Study,* published by Tecta in 1990. The text is based on the seminar "Fragment of an Enclave" given in Barcelona in 1985, which was then revised for lectures in Stockholm, 1986 and Beiging, 1987.
"TT1" refers to the Trundling Turk 1 lounge chair, designed in 1953 and produced by Tecta in 1983.

Alison Smithson, 12 November 1990

12/11/90

Dear Axel,
As I said, herewith corrected English text. Most pages look the same but there is one pair of facing sides without a picture. I will look in the [?].
There are ② [sketch of two folded pages] more folded pages necessary because of the length of the German text but all looks very good. Soraya & her family moved into their house (to camp!) Sunday and are very happy (so far) [text turns vertically to the side] (Because it is not cold weather)

Unsigned.

As with the previous postcard, Alison writes about the editing process of her book.
Soraya is Alison and Peter Smithsons' youngest daughter.

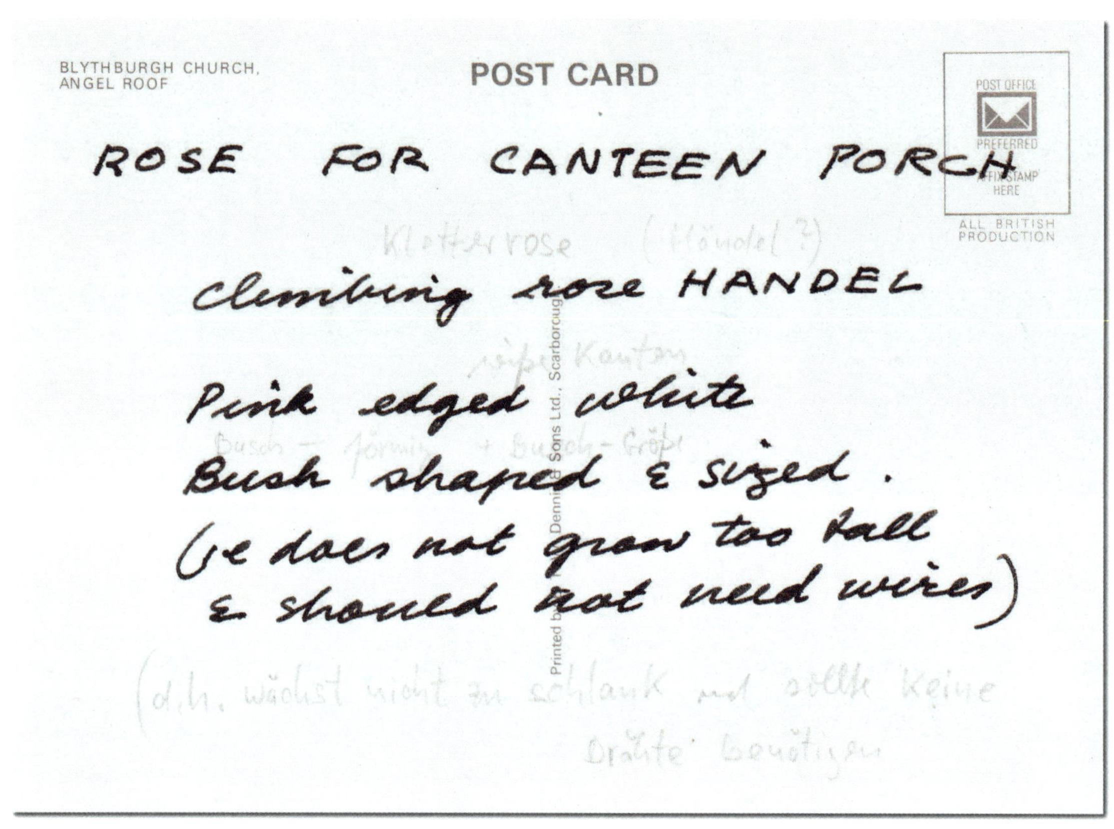

BLYTHBURGH CHURCH,
ANGEL ROOF

POST CARD

POST OFFICE
PREFERRED
AFFIX STAMP
HERE

ALL BRITISH
PRODUCTION

ROSE FOR CANTEEN PORCH
Kletterrose (Händel?)
climbing rose HANDEL
weiße Kanten
Pink edged white
Busch – förmig + Busch-Größe
Bush shaped & sized.
(ie does not grow too tall
& should not need wires)
(d.h. wächst nicht zu schlank und sollte keine
Drähte benötigen

Alison Smithson, undated / circa 1990

ROSE FOR CANTEEN PORCH
climbing rose HANDEL
Pink edged white
Bush shaped & sized. (ie does not grow too tall & should not need wires)

[added in pencil, probably Axel's own translation]:
Kletterrose (Händel?)
weiße Kanten
Busch – förmig + Busch – Größe
(d.h. wächst nicht zu schlank und sollte keine
Drähte benötigen)

Unsigned.

The project of the Tecta canteen porch dates from 1990. The postcard could be from that same year.

Alison Smithson, undated / circa 1990

Dear Axel, Roll will be posted today containing the paste-up that the printer should follow. I've made some notes for Otto on the 'spreads' and on a separate sheet. I've been looking through my ribbon oddments for cardinal red and at last found the colour among our Xmas wrappings. The sample is for colour, not for type, although 'cord' is nearer to the cords that hang from a cardinal's hat so perhaps we might consider it. I have no idea where the little piece came from, probably America. I think red will be more Tecta, don't you?

[A red satin cord is stapled to the postcard]

Unsigned.

The postcard must have been sent in 1990, while Alison was preparing *Saint Jerome; The Desert…The Study*, a publication for TECTA. The little book(let) is bound with a red satin thread. The paste-up document that Alison mentions is dated 1990, and the publication came out that same year.
"Otto" refers to Detlef Otto, a Tecta collaborator who assisted Alison with this publication and exhibition.

YU-CHEE CHONG

2 Whitehorse Street, Mayfair, London W1Y 7

Telephone: 01-491 3826

Maison Pagny of 99 faubourg St. Antoine, Paris (1865-1878)
Design for boulle semainier with one drawer for each day of the week, in ebony with brass inlay
Watercolour and encre de Chine wash with gum arabic
250 x 395mm

Alison Smithson, undated / circa 1990

Dear Axel
Thank you for the photographs of everything. I look forward to see the changed & changing light quality in your house. Peter will look at the Jerome chair when he is sorted out after being away. Maybe the seat should be a box-seat [schematic drawing] so as to give 'hat' shelf. I enclose the name/address of the Prouvé man connected with ILAUD Siena whom I mentioned: he told Peter, Piano wanted exhibition called 'Renzo Piano looks at Jean Prouvé'. Luckily Mme* looped the loop.
*daughter

[the description of the postcard "one drawer for each day of the week" is underlined and commented in pencil]
Why all the same then? It is a nice idea to follow Cornell boxes with Cornell drawers.

Unsigned.

The postcard could have been written after the Hexenhaus Holes were made in 1990, upon receiving photographs of the intervention from Axel.

Dear Axel, I enclose the name and
address of the architect
who researched Wohenbedarf: he says
they will have some Moser furniture
made in Italy soon but there are
hundreds of designs ---- also lamps
by Siegfried Gideon (and other things)
I was also shown a Jean Tinguely
catalogue with tiny wire models of
furniture which he made in
answer to Alexander Calder's
Circus (1950's?) Tinguely still working hard. I did not see Rüegg's
collection of furniture but others
said it spanned from Thonet to
Charlotte Perriand. He is a very nice
man. You might like
to contact him.

SIENA — Pinacoteca Nazionale
Sano di Pietro (Siena 1406 - Siena 1481) -
Santi Cosma e Damiano sostituiscono la gamba
malata del Diacono Giustiniano con quella tolta
ad un negro morto

Copyright by LOMBARDI, SIENA
Fotocolor Brassi

Alison Smithson, undated / circa 1990

Dear Axel, I enclose the name and address of the architect who researched Wohenbedarf: he says they will have some Moser furniture made in Italy soon but there are hundreds of designs ---- also lamps by Sigfried Gideon (and other things).
I was also shown a Jean Tinguely catalogue with tiny wire models of furniture which he made in answer to Alexander Calder's Circus (1950's?). Tinguely still working hard. I did not see Rüegg's collection of furniture but others said it spanned from Thonet to Charlotte Perriand. He is a very nice man. You might like [text turns vertically to the side] to contact him.

Unsigned.

Wohnbedarf means "housing needs", and was also the name of a Swiss furniture company launched by Sigfried Giedion, Werner Max Moser and Rudolf Garber in 1931.
"Rüegg" is a reference to Sergius Ruegenberg, who worked (mainly on furniture designs) in Mies van der Rohe's office in Berlin until 1937, when Mies moved to the United States. Axel Bruchhäuser contacted Ruegenberg because he was investigating Mies' furniture. Ruegenberg himself designed some chairs for Tecta in the 1980s.
The Swiss kinetic artist Jean Tinguely died in August 1991. The postcard was thus written before then.

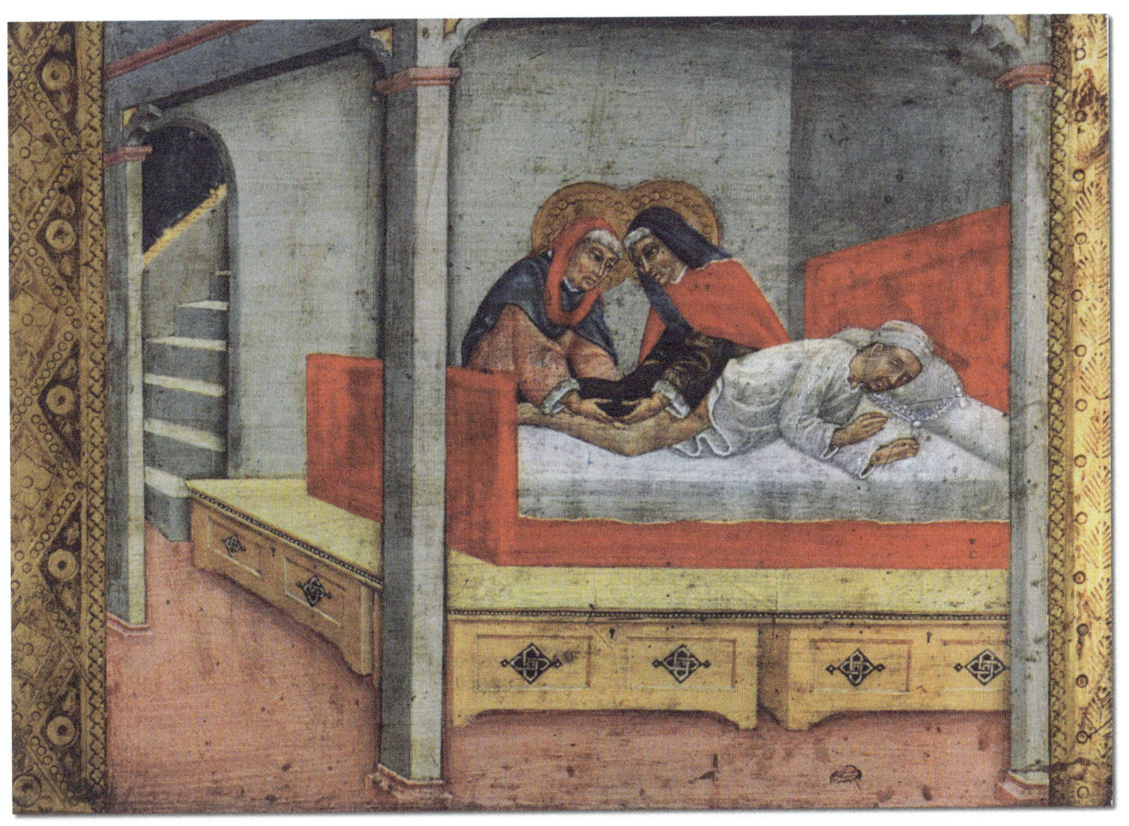

ALISON & PETER SMITHSON CATO LODGE 24 GILSTON ROAD LONDON SW10 9SR 01-373 7423

Dear Axel,
Herewith a drawing of the Angel table (that is as model 3 that I brought back).
There are 2 'jubilee' ecology signs: I will bring a print of each. Also there is being made a coloured axonometric of the Yellow Lookout. I will bring a colour xerox when I come.
I hope the kitchen tree is on its way.

13/5/91

Alison

Alison Smithson, 13 May 1991

13/5/91

Dear Axel,
Herewith a drawing of the Angel table (that is as model 3 that I brought back).
There are 2 'jubilee' ecology signs: I will bring a print of each. Also there is being made a coloured axonometric of the Yellow Lookout. I will bring a colour Xerox when I come. I hope the kitchen tree is on its way.
Alison

The Yellow Lookout is based on the Smithsons' entry for the Kingsbury Lookouts for the Landscape into Art competition, which was held in London in 1977. In 1984, Axel Bruchhäuser asked the Smithsons to design him a version of the lookout in the vicinity of the Hexenhaus. This was the Smithsons's first architectural commission from Bruchhäuser. Finally, some years and interventions later, the Yellow Lookout was lifted to the Tecta Courtyard in 1991. A hand-coloured copy of the Yellow lookout axonometry is now at the Tecta Gallery in Lauenförde.

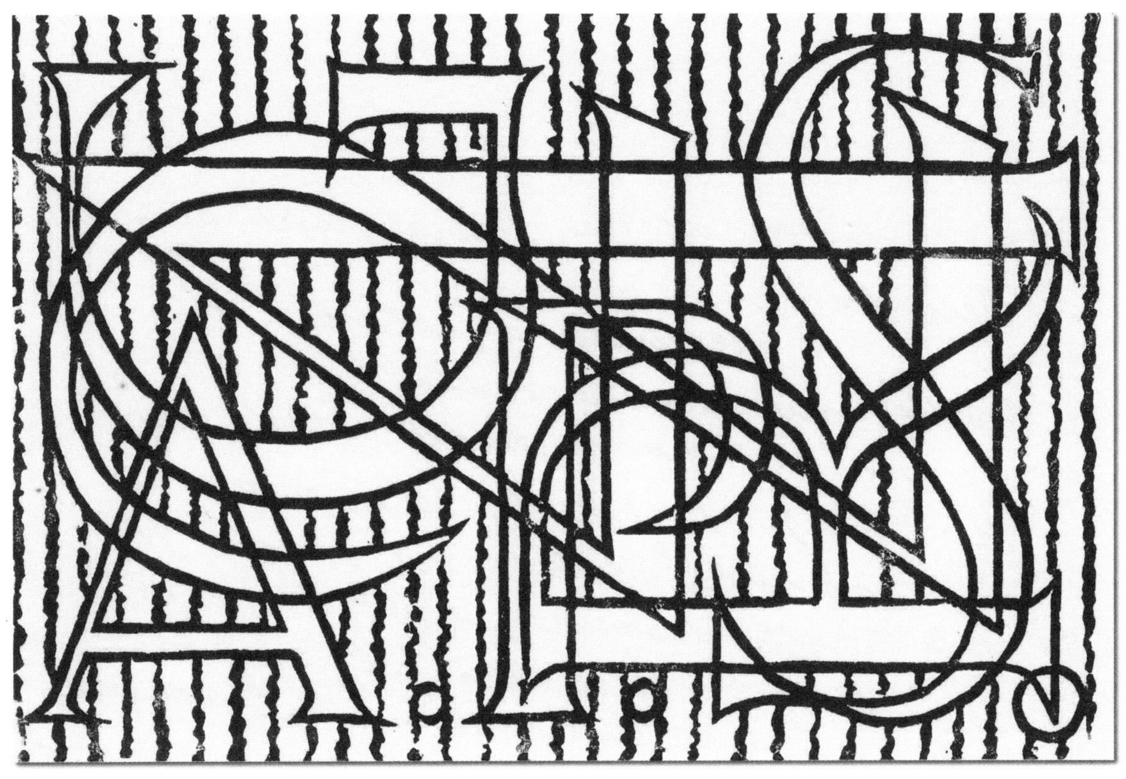

ALISON & PETER SMITHSON CATO LODGE 24 GILSTON ROAD LONDON SW10 9SR 01-373 7423

The drawings of the room will be sent this week.

Dear Axel,
Herewith a polaroid of mirror over consul table.
I am having a model made of the lamps to fit the silk pieces in the sample book and I will then test with a small light to find the effect: there seem at least 5 possible arrangements. But maybe this will not be accomplished until mid-October, after my return from U.S.
16/9/91
Alison.

Alison Smithson, 16 September 1991

The drawings of the room will be sent this week.

16/9/91

Dear Axel,
Herewith a polaroid of mirror over consul table.
I am having a model made of the lamps to fit the silk pieces in the sample book and I will then test with a small light to find the effect: there seem at least 5 possible arrangements.
But maybe this will not be accomplished until mid-October, after my return from U.S.
Alison

Alison refers to the Starfish Mirror accompanying her Consul Table design, 1991. A Starfish Mirror prototype can be found in the Hexenhaus bathroom.
The model for the lamp probably refers to the Silk Lantern, a floor lamp for Tecta, 1991 (Tecta catalogue, 1992).

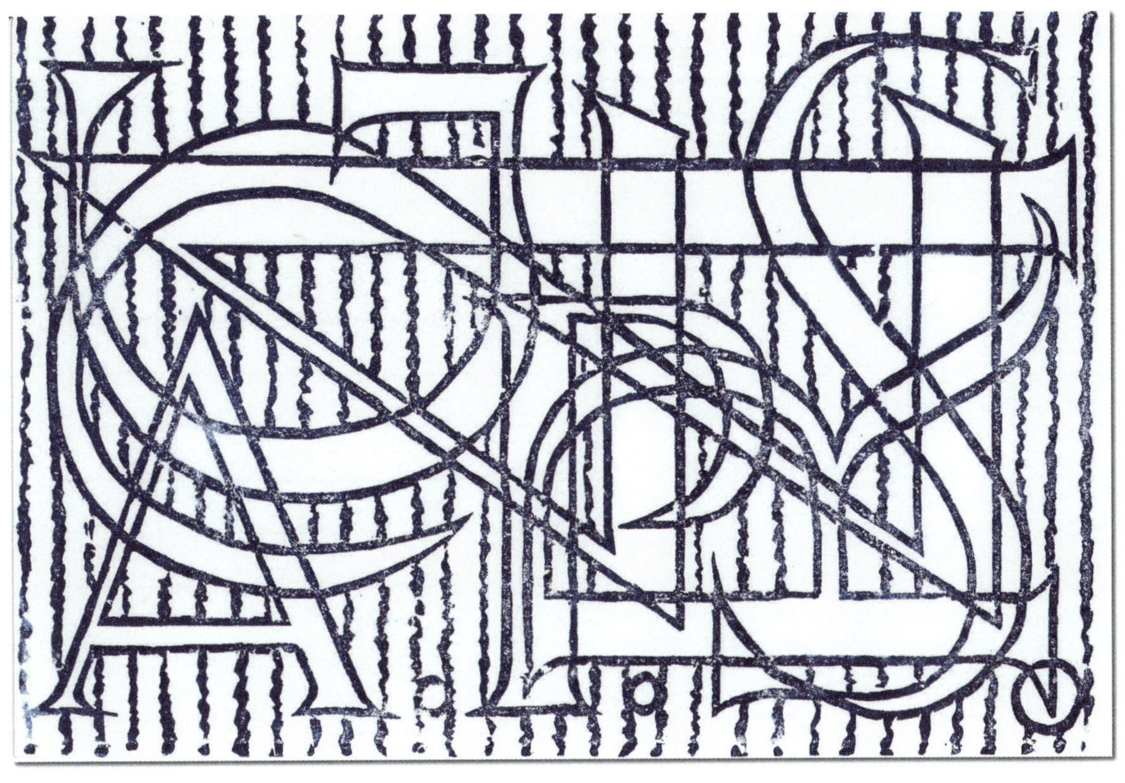

POST CARD

Name

Address

Shelving 1991 James Merriott M.A. (R.C.A.)
26 Bradley Close, London N7
071 609 3186 / 028 882 320

Printed by Thought Factory ® 40-42 Hastings Rd., Leicester. (0533) 765302

Alison Smithson, undated / circa 1991

Aeroplane shelves? No visible means of fixing vertical on wall.
RCA degree show

Unsigned.

The postcard is most likely from June 1991, as Alison mentions sending two postcards from the Royal College of Art Degree Show in a letter from 6 June 1991.

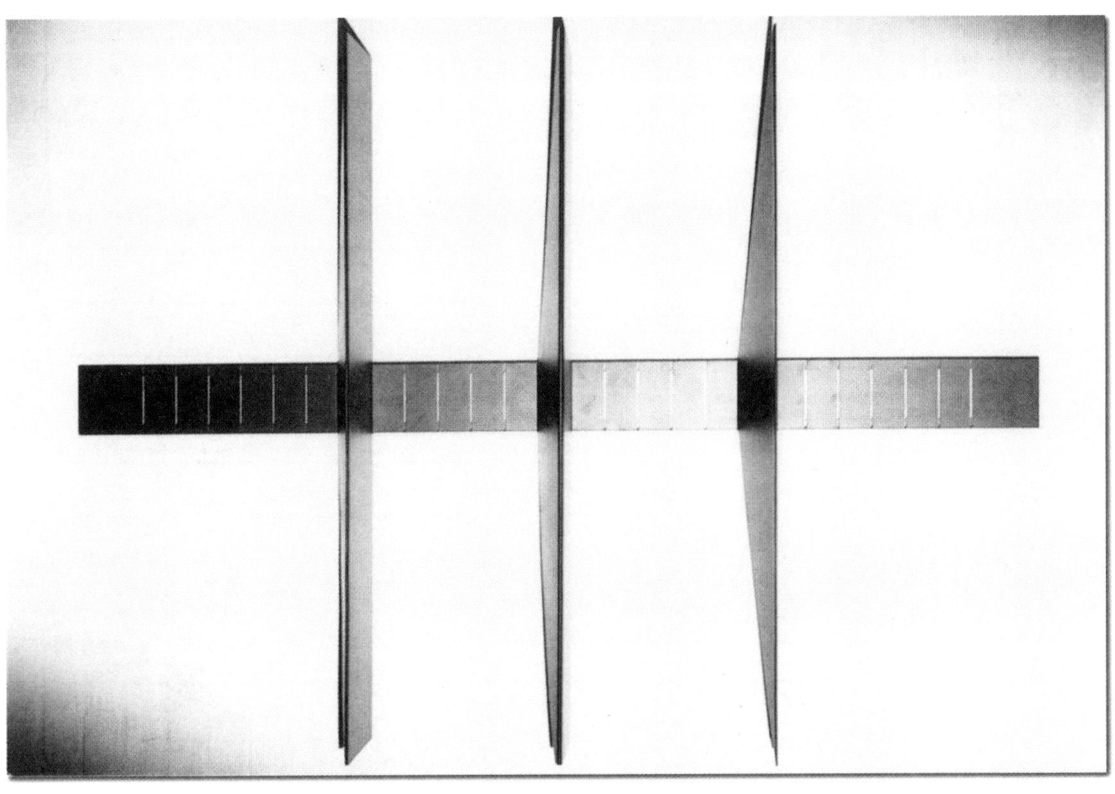

POST CARD

← 2 yellow 'webbing' straps one beside the other

← TOP METAL SLEEVE

← one strap behind other

seat had no single sheet edge & no reverse side showing Holes must have to do with folding machine

Name

Address

STRAP

STRAPS BETWEEN FIXING ON CEILING + FIXING ON FLOOR PLATE

∴ intended for use inside

← appeared 'glued' ∴ strap probably nylon.

Printed by Thought Factory ® 40-42 Hastings Rd., Leicester (0533) 765302

Aluminium Chair 1991
Tom Parker M.A. (R.C.A.).
Flat 3, 22 Fortess Road, NW5
071 - 267 4445 / 0622 - 890544

Alison Smithson, undated / circa 1991

[Sketch of a detail, annotated with arrows and text]

- 2 yellow 'webbing' straps one beside the other
- TOP METAL SLEEVE
- one strap behind other

[Sketch with arrows and text]

- STRAPS BETWEEN FIXING ON CEILING + FIXING ON FLOOR PLATE
- ∴ [therefore] intended for use inside
- appeared glued ∴ [therefore] strap probably nylon.

Seat had no single sheet edge & no reverse side showing
Holes must have to do with folding machine.

Unsigned.

The postcard is most likely from June 1991, as Alison mentions sending two postcards from the Royal College of Art Degree Show in a letter from 6 June 1991.

TECTA FURNITURE AT A.+P.S. EXHIBITION.

ALISON & PETER SMITHSON CATO LODGE 24 GILSTON ROAD LONDON SW10 9SR 01-373 7423

4/2/92

Dear Axel,

The furniture looked good in Stockholm (from where we have just returned). The exhibition goes to Copenhagen March 1st to 2nd so I have written to Jan Ahlstrand to let you know when/where the furniture should be collected. This is because the Italian shippers next take the exhibition panels to Turkey where I think the furniture should not go because of its bulk & probably no one has allowed for the extra cost.

Alison

Alison Smithson, 4 February 1992

TECTA FURNITURE AT A.+ P.S. EXHIBITION.

4/2/92

Dear Axel,
The furniture looked good in Stockholm (from where we have just returned). The exhibition goes to Copenhagen March 1st to 2nd so I have written to Jan Ahlstrand to let you know when/where the furniture should be collected. This is because the Italian shippers next take the exhibition panels to Turkey where I think the furniture should not go because of its bulk & probably no one has allowed for the extra cost.
Alison

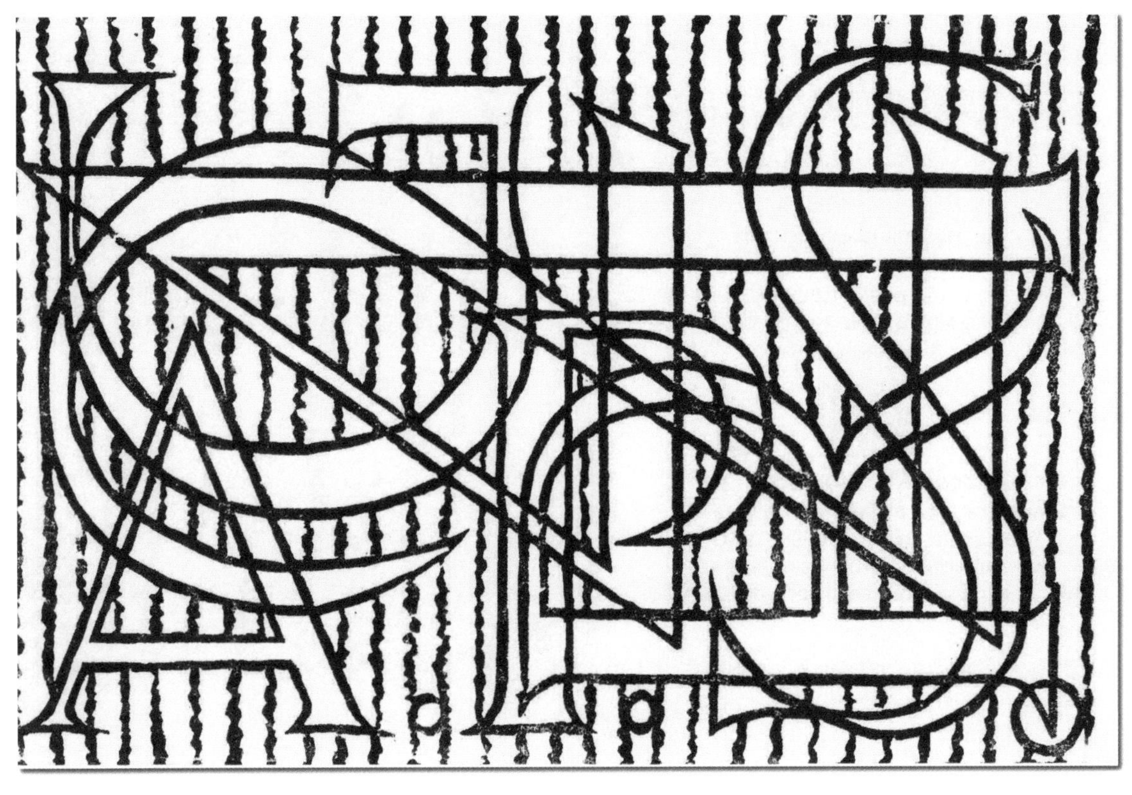

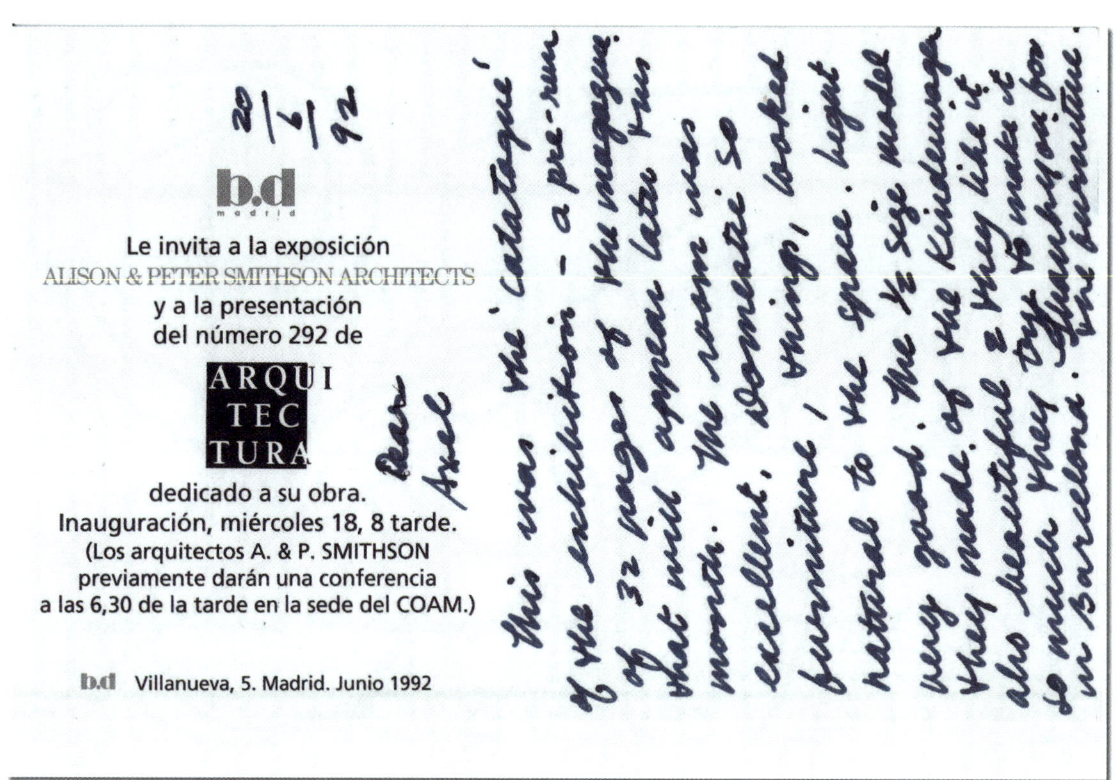

20/6/92

b.d
madrid

Le invita a la exposición
ALISON & PETER SMITHSON ARCHITECTS
y a la presentación
del número 292 de
ARQUI
TEC
TURA
dedicado a su obra.
Inauguración, miércoles 18, 8 tarde.
(Los arquitectos A. & P. SMITHSON
previamente darán una conferencia
a las 6,30 de la tarde en la sede del COAM.)

b.d Villanueva, 5. Madrid. Junio 1992

Alison Smithson, 20 June 1992

20/6/92

Dear Axel
This was the 'catalogue' of the exhibition — a pre-run of 32 pages of the magazine that will appear later this month. The room was excellent. Domestic so furniture, things, looked natural to the space. Height very good. The ½ size model they made of the Kinderwagen also beautiful & they like it so much they try to make it in Barcelona. Thank you for the furniture.

Unsigned.

The comments refer to the 1992 exhibition at b.d, a furniture and design gallery in Madrid.

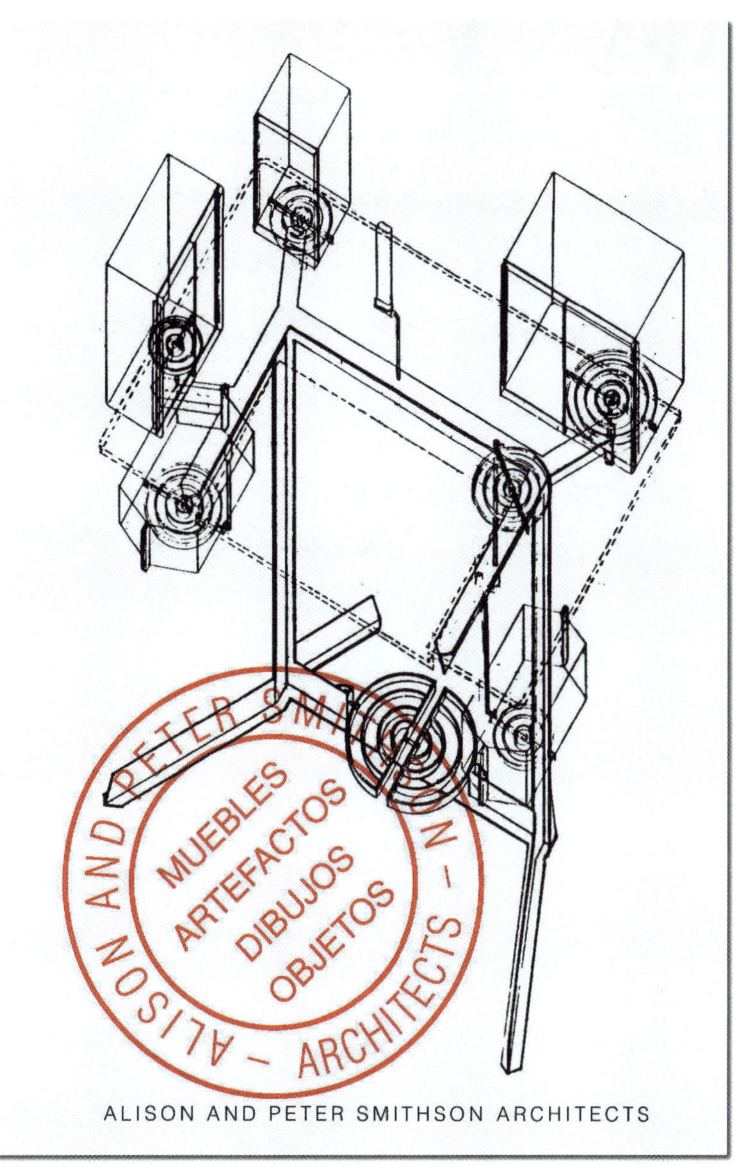
ALISON AND PETER SMITHSON - ARCHITECTS -
MUEBLES
ARTEFACTOS
DIBUJOS
OBJETOS
ALISON AND PETER SMITHSON ARCHITECTS

ZAMANA GALLERY

Zamana Gallery, 1 Cromwell Gardens, London SW7 2SL

MI 1

Dear Axel

29/6/92

I hope the enclosed notes are clear.
We await confirmation of the Cologne / Berlin dates ... or the cancellation of the idea.
Peter reads the Brothers Grimm.
I'm on the run...
I'll be in touch, if need be, after Hungary.

Alison

The observatory's armillary spheres.
Jaipur, Rajasthan
©1986 Roland & Sabrina Michaud/
The John Hillelson Agency Ltd.

Alison Smithson, 29 June 1992

29/6/92

Dear Axel,
I hope the enclosed notes are clear. We await confirmation of the Cologne / Berlin dates… or the cancellation of the idea. Peter reads the Brothers Grimm. I'm on the run…
I'll be in touch, if need be, after Hungary.
Alison

In early 1993, the Smithsons (together with Tecta) took their exhibition *Tischlein deck dich* to the Mautsch Gallery, Cologne (in January) and to Aedes Gallery, Berlin (in February). Alison could not attend the Berlin exhibition as she was already gravely ill.

Dear Axel,

Thank you for the 'diapositives'/slide films of the new works.

Do you have a print of a plan of the whole of the factory?

We want to try a drawing with all the small additions added to the plan (for publication purposes)

Alison

26/8/92

b.d madrid

Le invita a la exposición

ALISON & PETER SMITHSON ARCHITECTS

y a la presentación

del número 292 de

ARQUI
TEC
TURA

dedicado a su obra.

Inauguración, miércoles 18, 8 tarde.

(Los arquitectos A. & P. SMITHSON

previamente darán una conferencia

a las 6,30 de la tarde en la sede del COAM.)

b.d Villanueva, 5. Madrid. Junio 1992

Alison Smithson, August 26, 1992

26/8/92

Dear Axel,
Thank you for the 'diapositives'/ slide films of the new works.
Do you have a print of <u>a plan of the whole of the factory?</u>
We want to try a drawing with all the small additions added to the plan (for publication purposes)
Alison

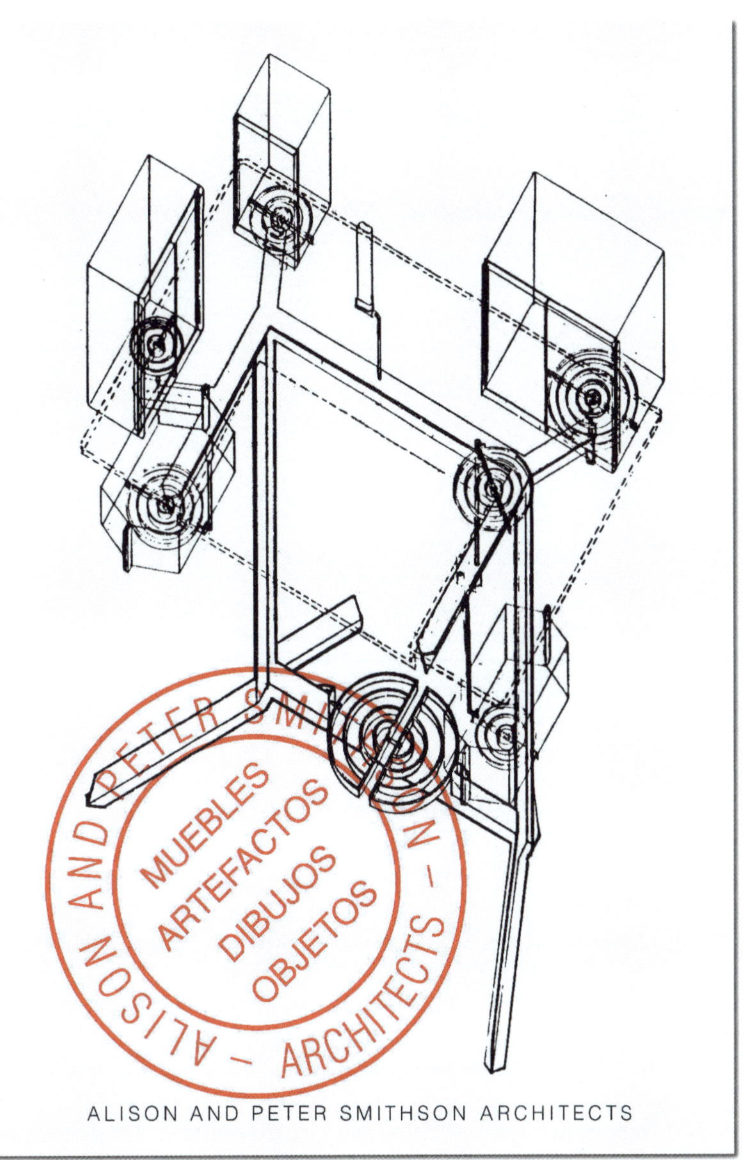
ALISON AND PETER SMITHSON - ARCHITECTS -
MUEBLES
ARTEFACTOS
DIBUJOS
OBJETOS
ALISON AND PETER SMITHSON ARCHITECTS

would you please choose the train
time from Regensburg to suit a good
time to pick me up.
Do you need more wood fruit? I
have found another source but the
fruits are about £2.50 each: more
expensive.
Have you arranged to pick up
the furniture from Aahlstrand?
It was nice watching young people
using TT1: walking themselves
around the floor, etc.
I look forward to the gate.
Mice to Karlchen. Alison

Alison Smithson, undated / circa 1992

Dear Axel,
Thank you for my photograph.
To confirm: arriving by train from Regensburg to Göttingen Tuesday May 19th
departing by train to Frankfurt airport Sunday May 24th
Nearer to the date, would you please choose the train time from Regensburg to suit a good time to pick me up.
Do you need more wood fruit? I have found another source but the fruits are about £2.50 each: more expensive.
Have you arranged to pick up the furniture from Aahlstrand? It was nice watching young people using TT1: walking themselves around the floor, etc.
I look forward to the gate.
Mice to Karlchen. Alison

Alison makes reference to the wooden, painted fruit used in the *Tischlein deck dich* exhibition which showcased some Tecta furniture. It was held at Mautsch Gallery in Cologne and then Aedes Gallery in Berlin, in early 1993.
The “gate” in question refers to the new gate design (1992) for the Tecta premises. This postcard could therefore be from 1992.

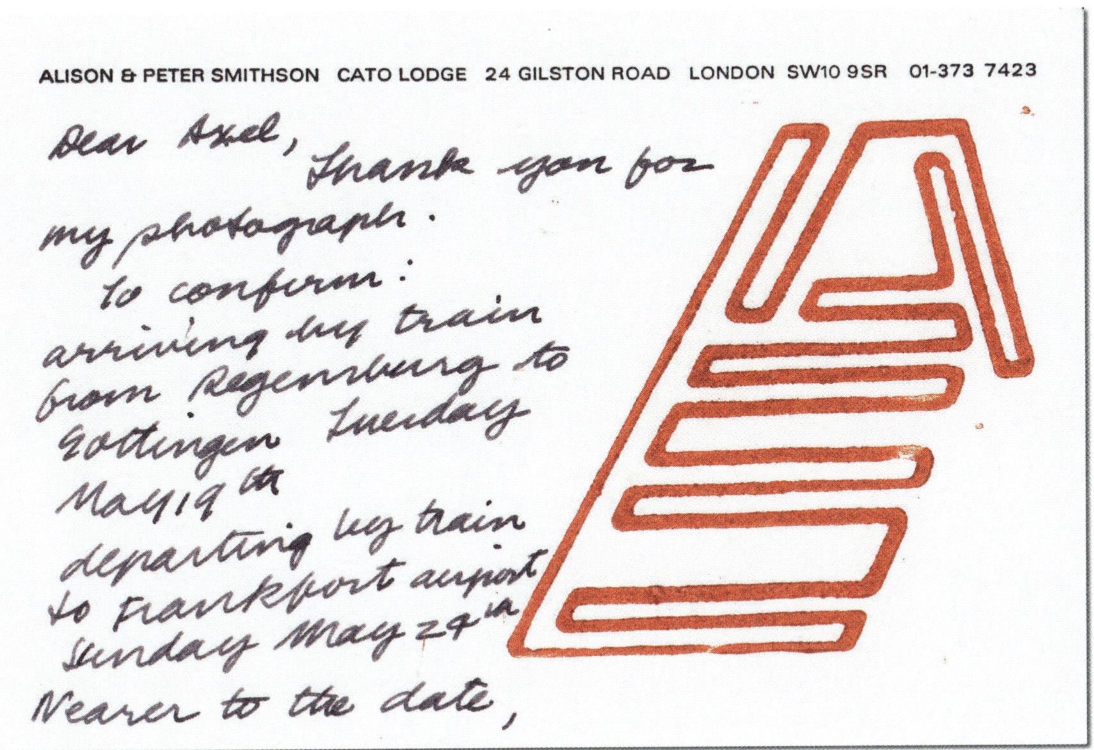

ALISON & PETER SMITHSON CATO LODGE 24 GILSTON ROAD LONDON SW10 9SR 01-373 7423

Dear Axel,
Thank you for
my photograph.
to confirm:
arriving by train
from Regensburg to
Göttingen Tuesday
May 19th
departing by train
to Frankfurt airport
Sunday May 24th
Nearer to the date,

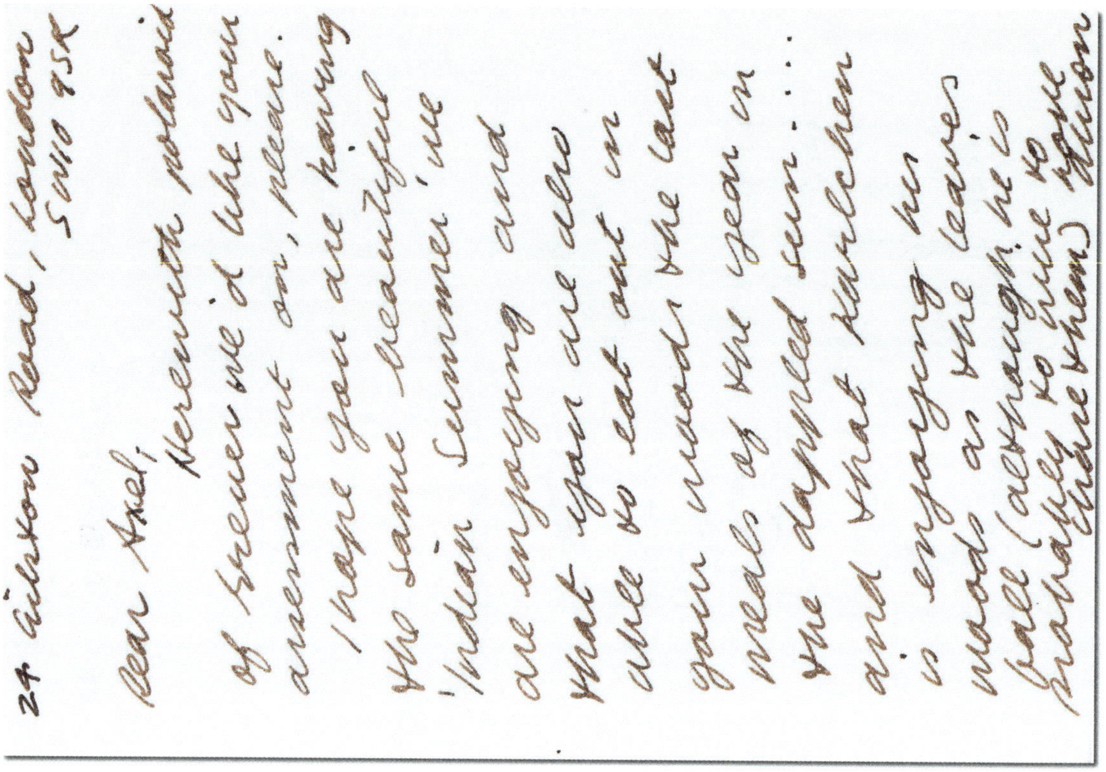

Alison Smithson, undated / circa 1992

24 Gilston Road, London
SW10 9SR

Dear Axel,
Herewith polaroid of Breuer we'd like your assessment on, please. I hope you are having the same beautiful 'Indian summer' we are enjoying and that you are also able to eat out in your woods the last meals of the year in the dappled sun… and that Karlchen is enjoying his woods as the leaves fall (although he is to[o] nice to chase them)
Love Alison

The drawing on the postcard is a scheme for the design of the Wide-Shouldered Office Chair that Alison and Axel were working on in 1992. The postcard could be from the same year.

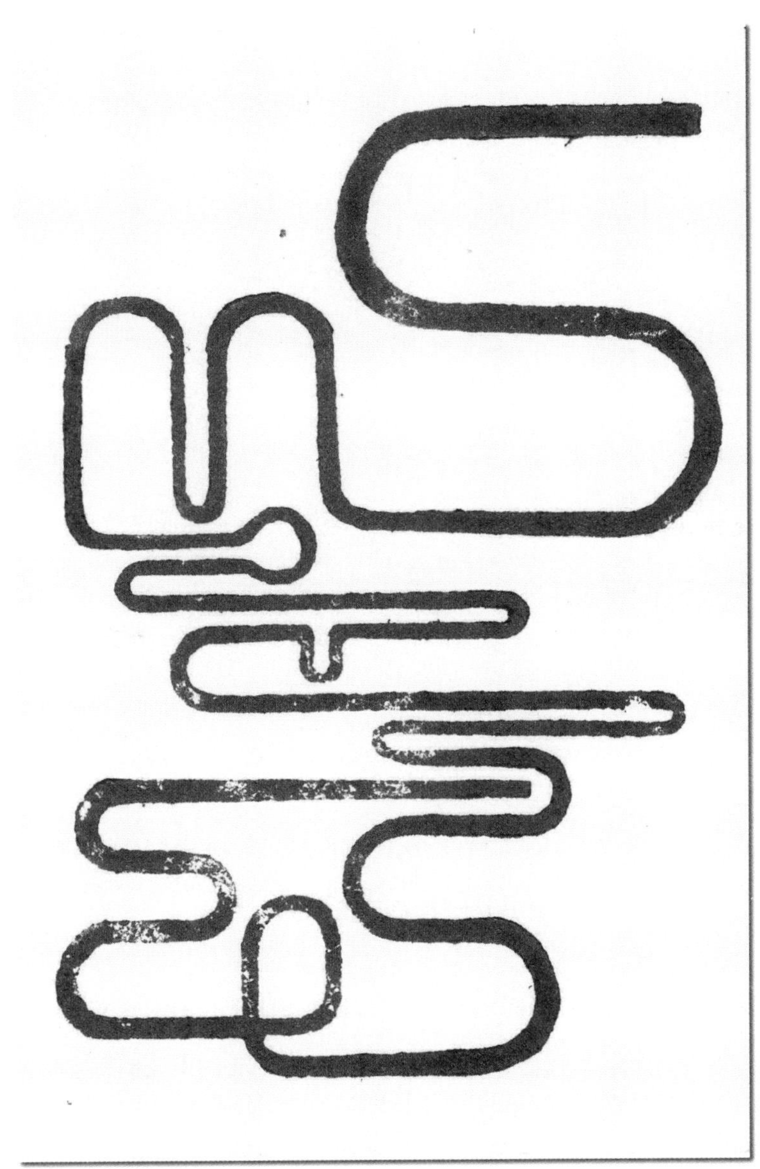

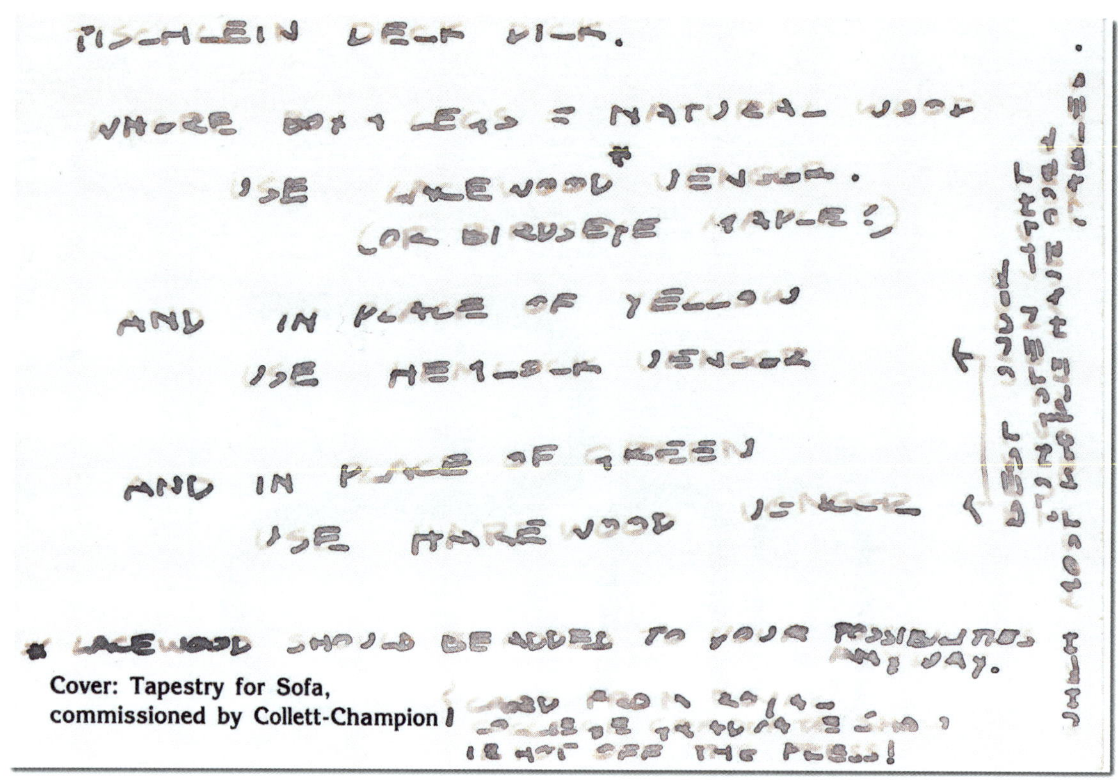

Alison Smithson, undated / circa 1992

TISCHLEIN DECK DICK.
WHERE BOX + LEGS = NATURAL WOOD USE LACEWOOD* VENEER (OR BIRDSEYE MAPLE?)
AND IN PLACE OF YELLOW USE HEMLOCK VENEER
AND IN PLACE OF GREEN USE HAREWOOD VENEER

*LACEWOOD SHOULD BE ADDED TO YOUR POSSIBILITIES ANYWAY.

[Vertical text with arrows pointing to harewood veneer and hemlock veneer]: BEST UNDER TUNGSTEN LIGHT WHICH MOST PEOPLE HAVE OVER TABLES.

[Note at the bottom]:
CARD FROM ROYAL
COLLEGE GRADUATE SHOW
IE HOT OFF THE PRESS!

Unsigned.

The postcard must be from late 1992. The comments refer to the Tischlein deck dich table, designed by Tecta with Alison's assistance. The table was made for the aforementioned *Tischlein deck dich* exhibition.

KELLY-ANNE FLETCHER

Tapestry Weaver

081 802 2214

Alison Smithson, 29 April 1993

29/4/93

Dear Axel,
I send you this article with pictures because my instinct tells me that Rietvelt saw illustrations — probably fairly crude line drawings, even engraved — of this or similar Godwin pieces in a Dutch trade journal for carpenters / joiners / furniture makers. I became interested in Godwin as a student because of the Japanese influence. (The Rietvelt big yellow catalogue is tedious!)

Unsigned.

Edward William Godwin (1833-86) was a British architect, designer and writer, notable for his contributions to the British Aesthetic movement.
An exemplar of the Rietveld design is now placed at the Hexenhaus. The “big yellow catalogue” Alison refers to is Marijke Küper, Marijke and Ada Van Zijl, Ada (eds.), *Gerrit Th. Rietveld 1888-1964: L'oeuvre complet*, Utrecht: Centraal Museum, 1993.

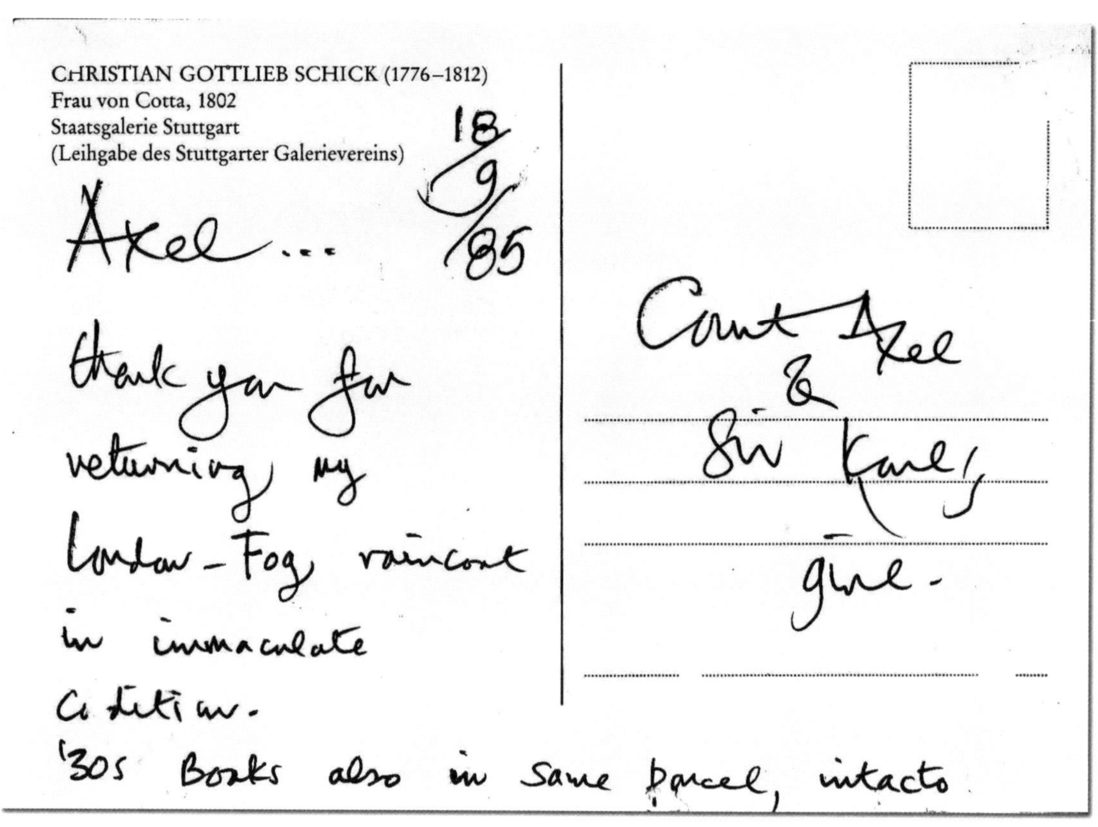

CHRISTIAN GOTTLIEB SCHICK (1776–1812)
Frau von Cotta, 1802
Staatsgalerie Stuttgart
(Leihgabe des Stuttgarter Galerievereins)

18/9/85

Axel...

thank you for returning my London-Fog raincoat in immaculate condition.
'30s Books also in same parcel, intacto.

Count Axel & Sir Karl's girl.

Peter Smithson, 18 September 1985

18/9/85

Count Axel & Sir Karl's girl.

Axel...
Thank you for returning my London-Fog raincoat in immaculate condition.
'30s Books also in same parcel, intacto.

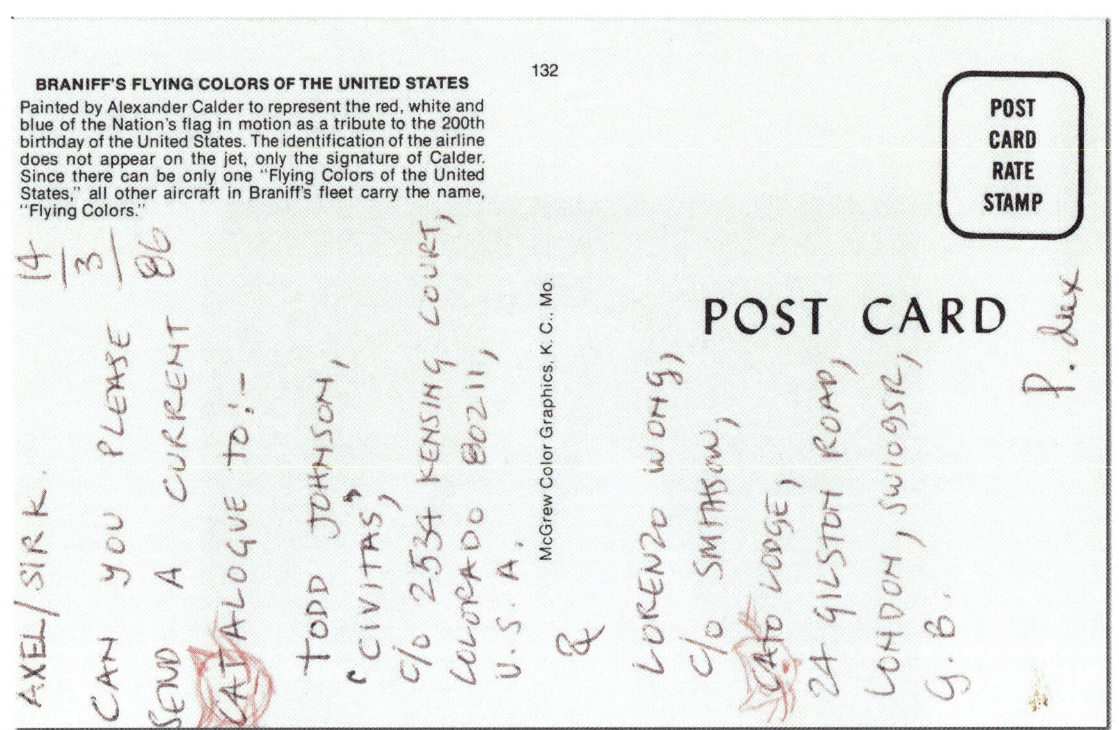

Peter Smithson, 14 March 1986

14/3/86

AXEL / SIR K.
CAN YOU PLEASE SEND A CURRENT
CATALOGUE TO:
TODD JOHNSON,
'CIVITAS',
C/O 2534 KENSING COURT,
COLORADO 80211,
U.S.A.
&
LORENZO WONG,
C/O SMITHSON,
CATO LODGE
24 GILSTON ROAD,
LONDON, SW10 9SR,
G.B.

P. dux

Here, Peter signs as P. dux, instead of his usual P.S. This is perhaps because another P.S. — Peter Salter — was working in the studio at the time. "Dux" is a Scottish term for "top pupil", and/or a Saxon term meaning "chief" or "leader".

BI

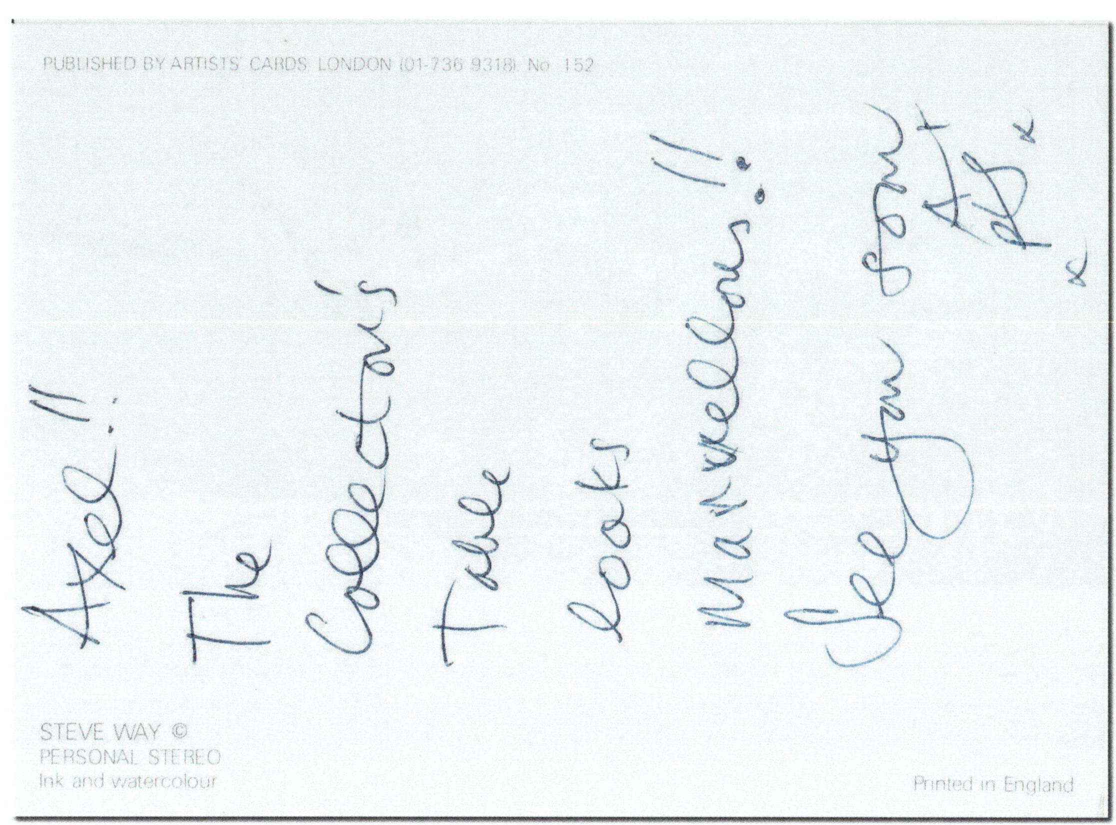

Peter Smithson, undated / circa 1989

Axel!!
The
Collector's
Table
looks
marvellous!!
See you soon
A+PS x x

The Collector's Table was designed by Alison in 1986, and featured in the Tecta catalogue in 1987 and 1992. It was also exhibited in the *Tischlein deck dich* exhibition (1993) in Cologne and Berlin. The official photographs that Peter is probably referring to here, with a Cato Lodge stamp and date, are from 1989.

WALKMAN

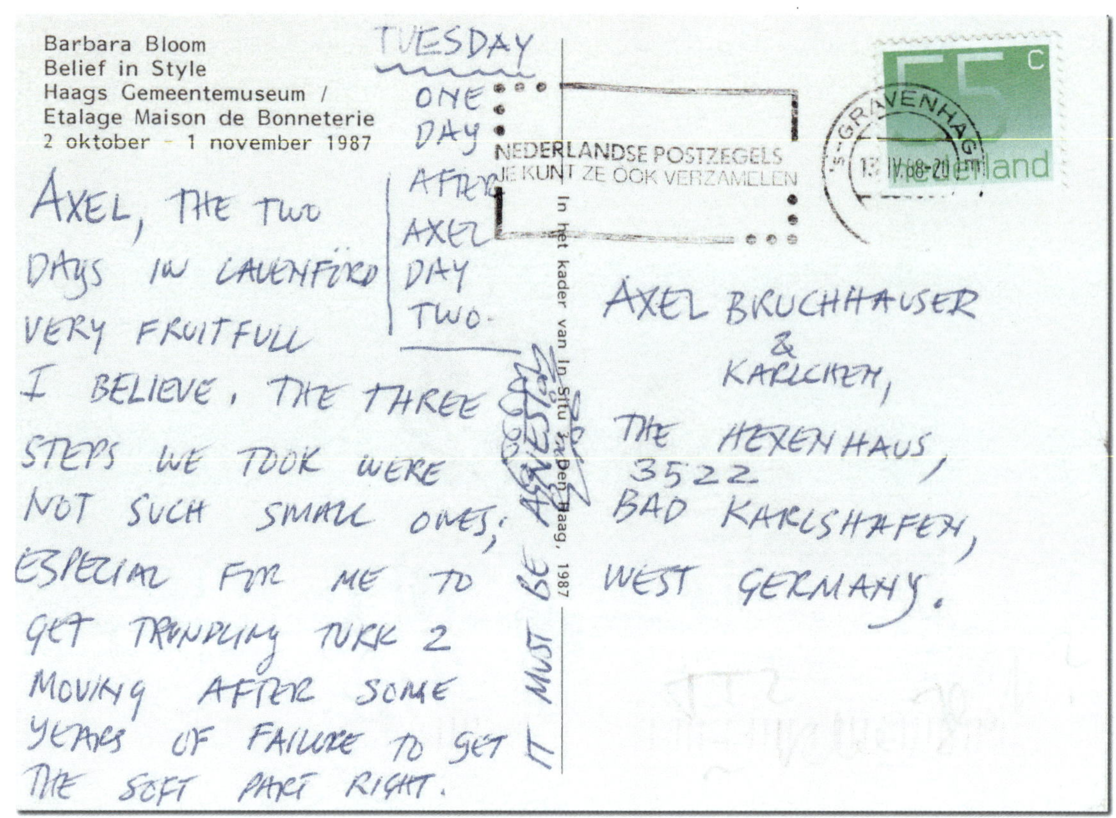

Barbara Bloom
Belief in Style
Haags Gemeentemuseum /
Etalage Maison de Bonneterie
2 oktober - 1 november 1987
NEDERLANDSE POSTZEGELS
JE KUNT ZE OOK VERZAMELEN
In het kader van In Situ in Den Haag, 1987
's-GRAVENHAGE
13.IV.88-20
55 c
nederland
AXEL BRUCHHAUSER
&
KARLCHEN,
THE HEXENHAUS,
3522
BAD KARLSHAFEN,
WEST GERMANY.

Peter Smithson, 13 April 1988

[Stamp] GRAVENHAGE 13.IV.88-20

AXEL, THE TWO	<u>TUESDAY</u>
DAYS IN LAUENFÖRD	ONE
VERY FRUITFULL	DAY
I BELIEVE, THE THREE	AFTER
STEPS WE TOOK WERE	AXEL
NOT SUCH SMALL ONES;	DAY
ESPECIAL FOR ME	TWO.
TO GET TRUNDLING TURK 2	
MOVING AFTER SOME	
YEARS OF FAILURE TO GET	
THE SOFT PART RIGHT.	

[Text continues vertically]
IT MUST BE A NEST [upon a doodle of a nest]

Unsigned.

The Trundling Turk II was a 1976 version of the lounge chair with an external chassis. A Tecta prototype was made in 1987, with an ikat fabric. This prototype is now placed in the Hexenhaus. Several units were produced, but the design was never included in the Tecta Catalogue. It was, however, exhibited at the Cologne International Furniture Fair in 1991.

BELIEF IN STYLE

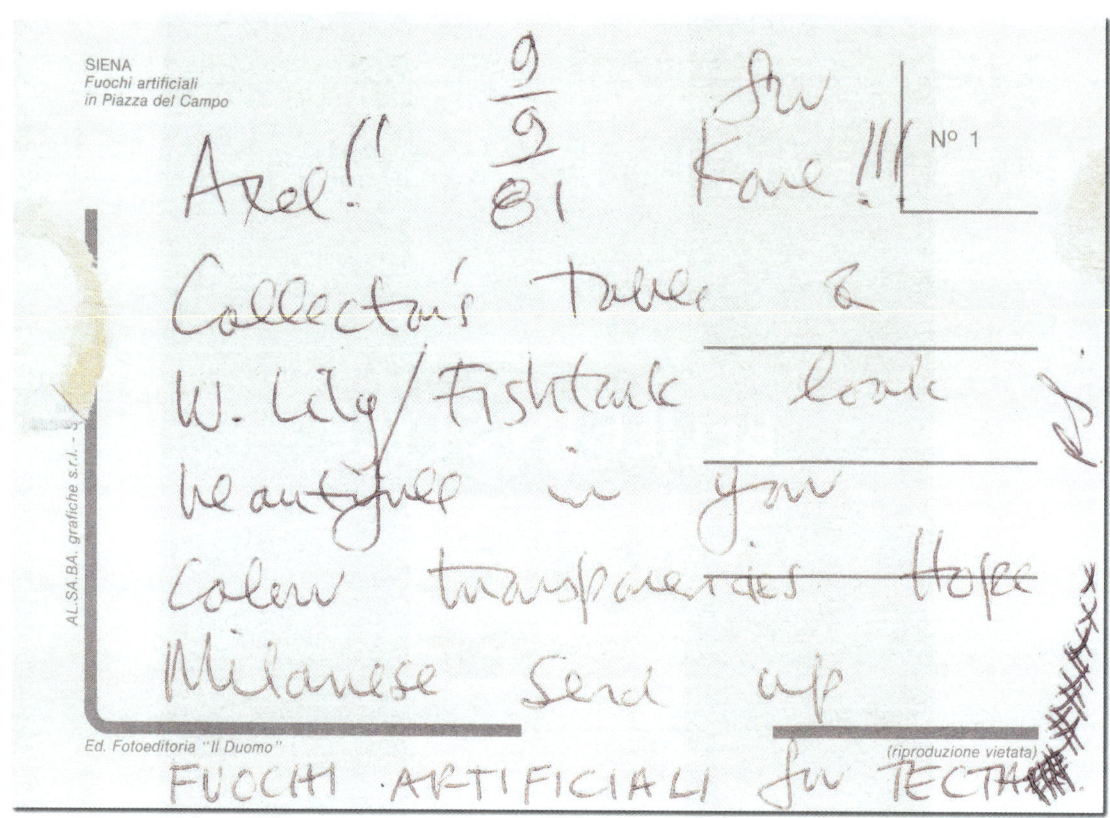

Peter Smithson, 9 September [1981]; circa 1991

9/9/81

Axel!! & Karl!!!
The
Collector's Table & W. Lily / Fishtable look
beautifull in your
colour transparencies. Hope
Milanese send up
FUOCHI ARTIFICIALI for TECTA
xxxxxxxxxxxxxxxxx
PS.

Wrongly dated. The Collector's Table and the Waterlily and Fish desk were exhibited at the Milan furniture fair in 1991. The postcard is likely to be from September of that same year.

SIENA

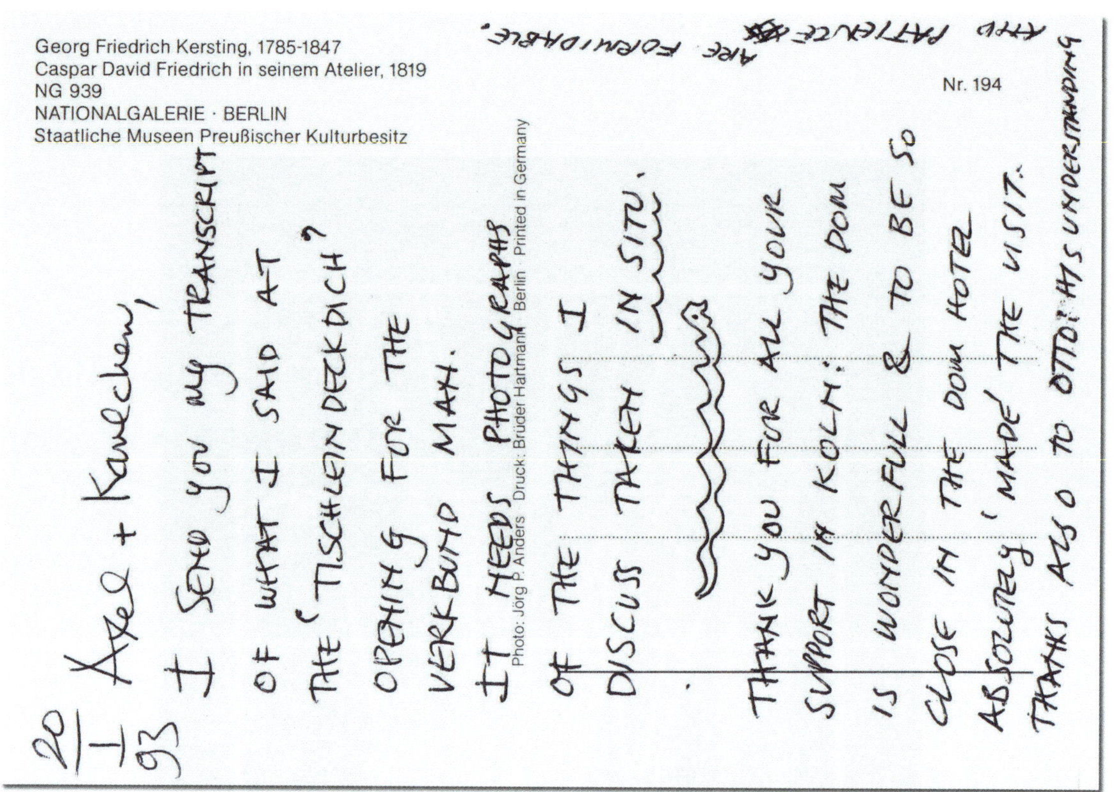

Peter Smithson, 20 January 1993

20/1/93

Axel + Karlchen,
I SEND YOU MY TRANSCRIPT
OF WHAT I SAID AT 'TISCHLEIN DECK DICH'
OPENING FOR THE
VERKBUND MAN.
IT NEEDS PHOTOGRAPHS
OF THE THINGS I
DISCUSS TAKEN IN SITU.
[a doodle of a snake]
THANK YOU FOR ALL YOUR
SUPPORT IN KOLN: THE DOM
IS WONDERFULL & TO BE SO
CLOSE IN THE DOM HOTEL
ABSOLUTELY 'MADE' THE VISIT.
THANKS ALSO TO OTTO: HIS UNDERSTANDING
[text continues vertically] AND PATIENCE ARE FORMIDABLE.

Unsigned.

Tecta brought the *Tischlein deck dich* exhibition to Mautsch Gallery in Cologne. Peter gave a speech at the inauguration of the exhibition, which had been designed by Alison.

b.d
madrid

Le invita a la exposición
ALISON & PETER SMITHSON ARCHITECTS
y a la presentación
del número 292 de
ARQUI
TEC
TURA
dedicado a su obra.
Inauguración, miércoles 18, 8 tarde.
(Los arquitectos A. & P. SMITHSON
previamente darán una conferencia
a las 6,30 de la tarde en la sede del COAM.)

b.d Villanueva, 5. Madrid. Junio 1992

18/2/93
Axel … Karlchen,
Here is text of
what I said, not very
well, at the Galerie
Aedes. It went off well.
thank-you for all your help
(and companionship of course)
P.S.
A.S. thought the little book lovely

Peter Smithson, 18 February 1993

18/2/93

Axel… Karlchen,
Here is text of
what I said, not very
well, at the Galerie
Aedes. It went off well.
Thank you for all your help
(and companionship of course)
P.S.
[Written to the side of the postcard]:
A.S. thought the little book lovely.

After Cologne, the exhibition travelled to the Aedes Gallery in Berlin. Peter again gave a speech at the inauguration, on 15 February. Alison was already seriously ill and could not travel.

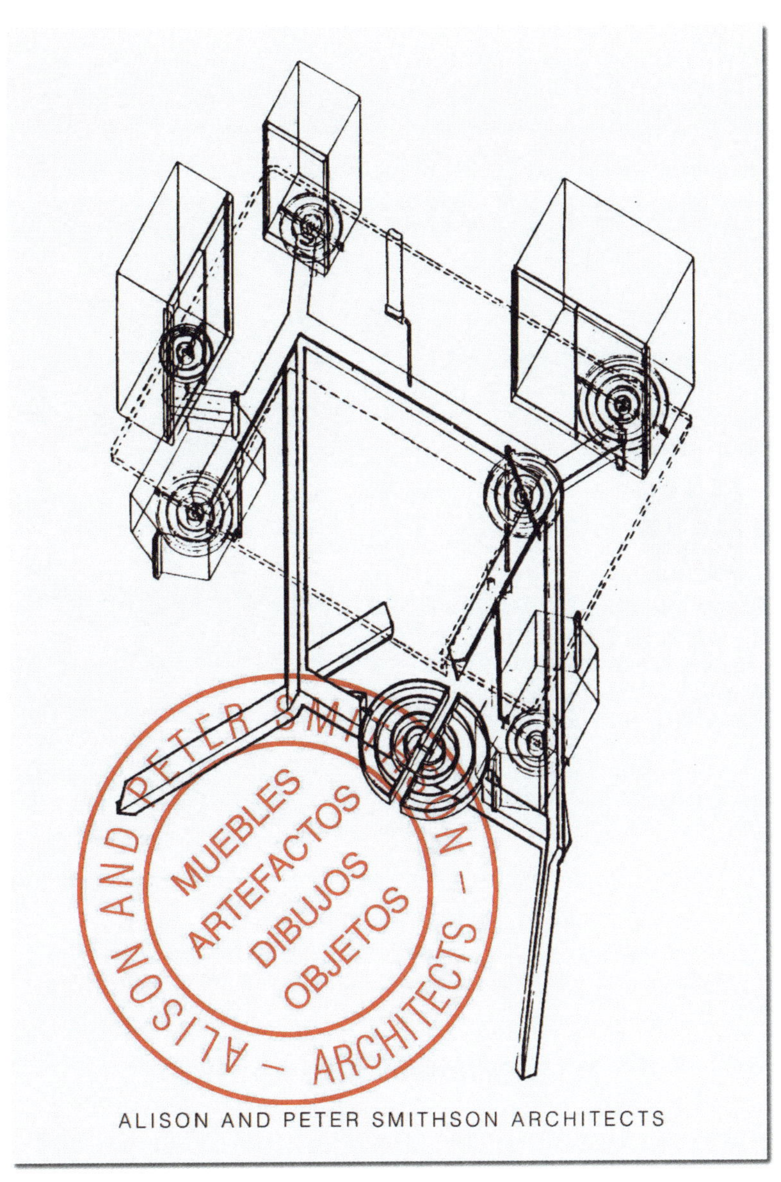
ALISON AND PETER SMITHSON – ARCHITECTS –
MUEBLES
ARTEFACTOS
DIBUJOS
OBJETOS
ALISON AND PETER SMITHSON ARCHITECTS

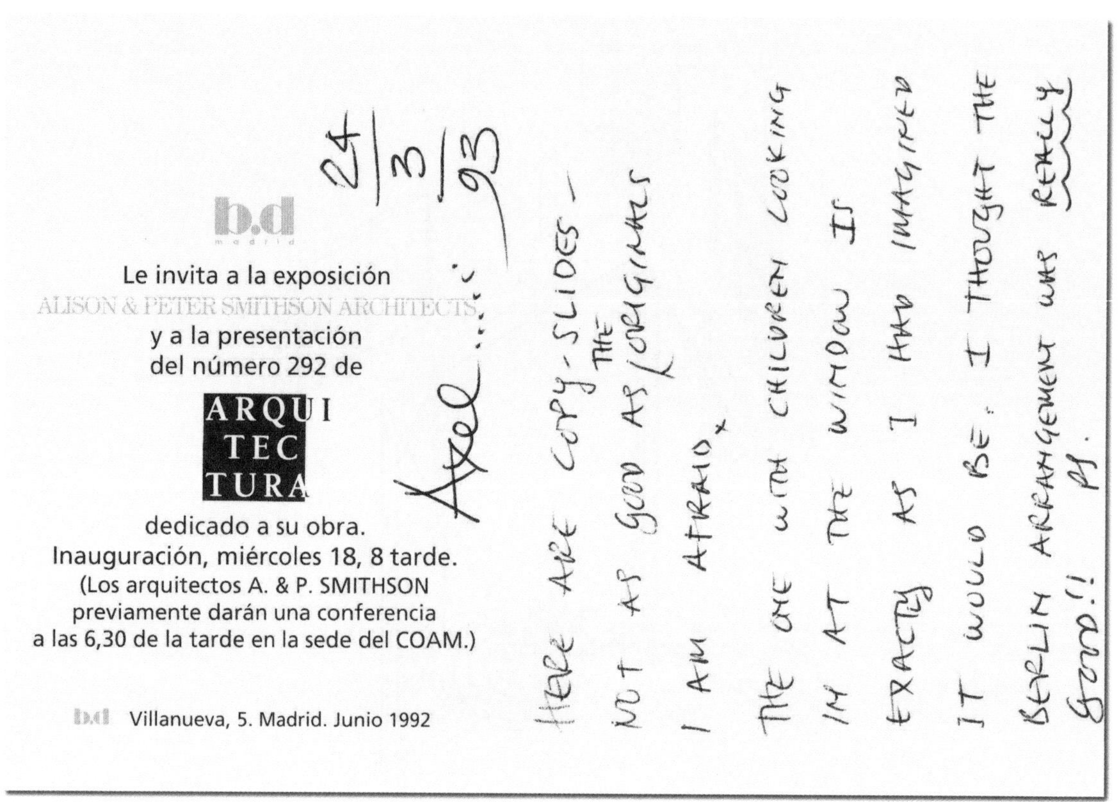

Peter Smithson, 24 March 1993

24/3/93

Axel......
HERE ARE COPY-SLIDES –
NOT AS GOOD AS THE ORIGINALS
I AM AFRAID.
THE ONE WITH CHILDREN LOOKING
IN AT THE WINDOW IS
EXACTLY AS I HAD IMAGINED
IT WOULD BE. I THOUGHT THE
BERLIN ARRANGEMENT WAS REALLY
GOOD!! PS.

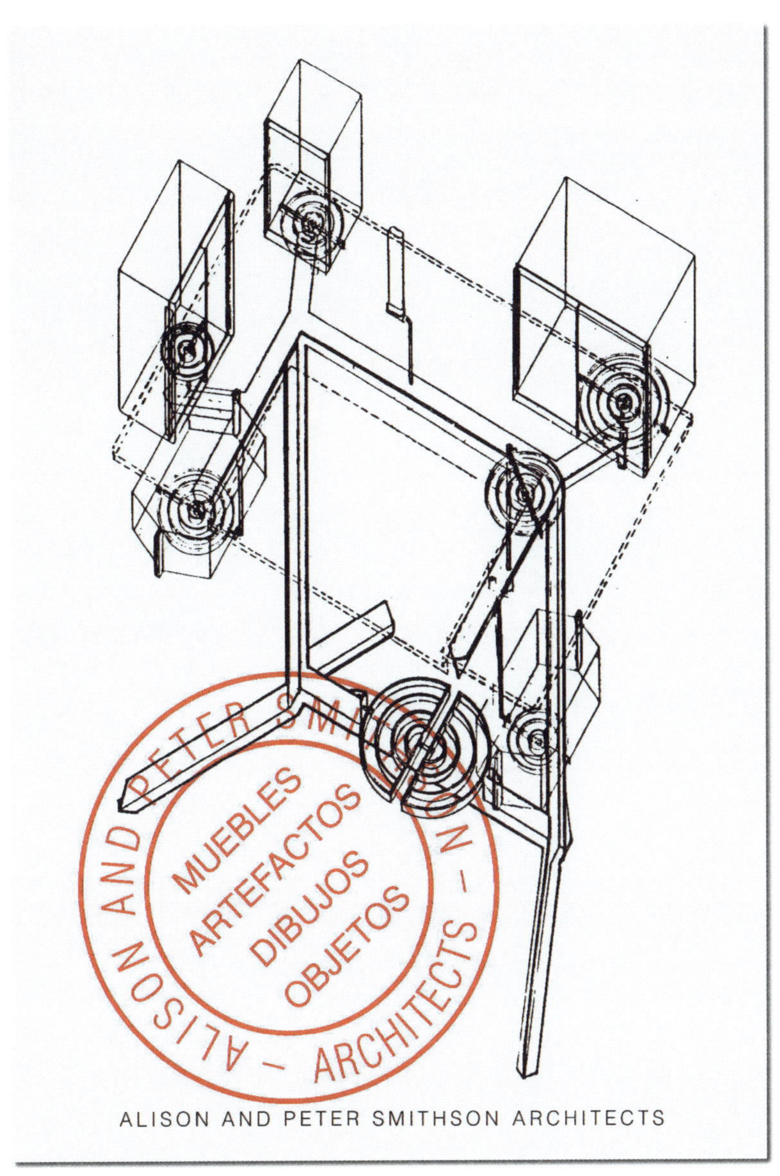
ALISON AND PETER SMITHSON - ARCHITECTS -
MUEBLES
ARTEFACTOS
DIBUJOS
OBJETOS
ALISON AND PETER SMITHSON ARCHITECTS

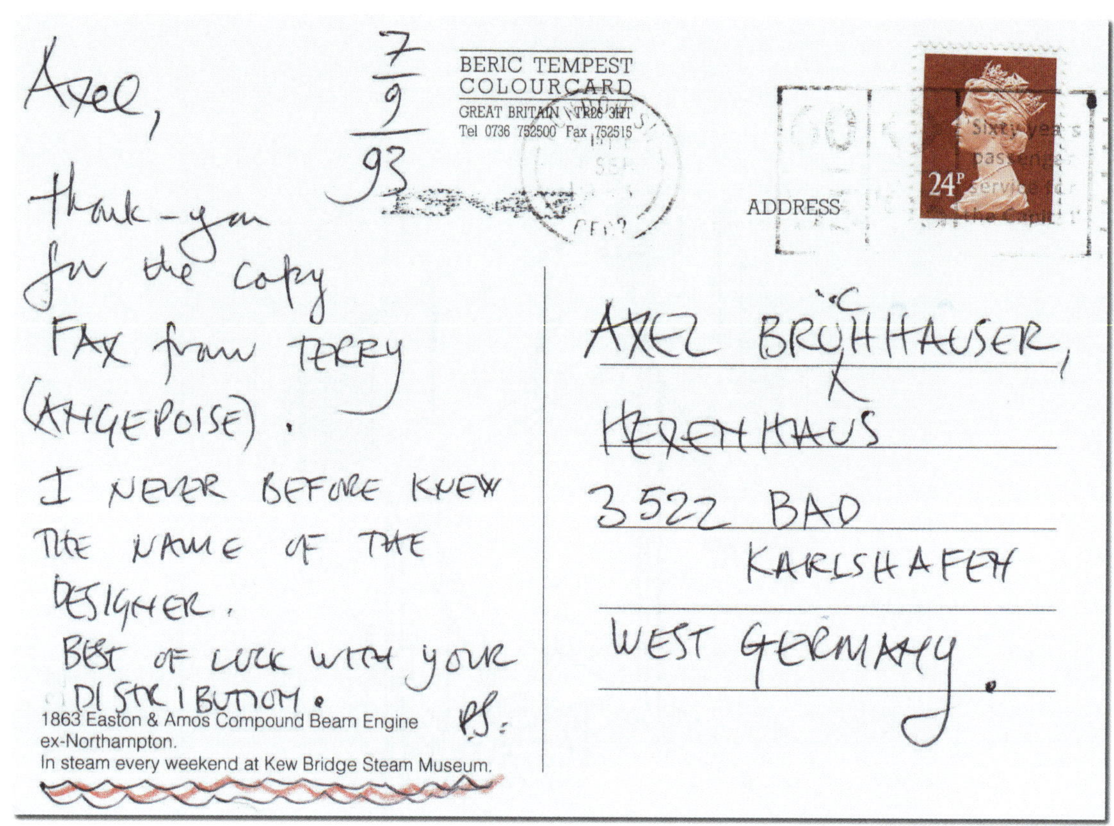
7/9/93

Axel,

thank-you for the copy FAX from TERRY (ANGLEPOISE).

I NEVER BEFORE KNEW THE NAME OF THE DESIGNER.

BEST OF LUCK WITH YOUR DISTRIBUTION.

P.S.

BERIC TEMPEST COLOURCARD
GREAT BRITAIN TR26 3HT
Tel 0736 752500 Fax 752515

ADDRESS

AXEL BRÜHHAUSER,
HERENHAUS
3522 BAD KARLSHAFEN
WEST GERMANY.

1863 Easton & Amos Compound Beam Engine ex-Northampton.
In steam every weekend at Kew Bridge Steam Museum.

Peter Smithson, 7 September 1993

7/9/93

Axel,
Thank you
for the copy
FAX from TERRY
(ANGLEPOISE).
I NEVER BEFORE KNEW
THE NAME OF THE
DESIGNER.
BEST OF LUCK WITH YOUR
DISTRIBUTION.
P.S.

The Terry family owns and manages the classic Anglepoise lighting firm.

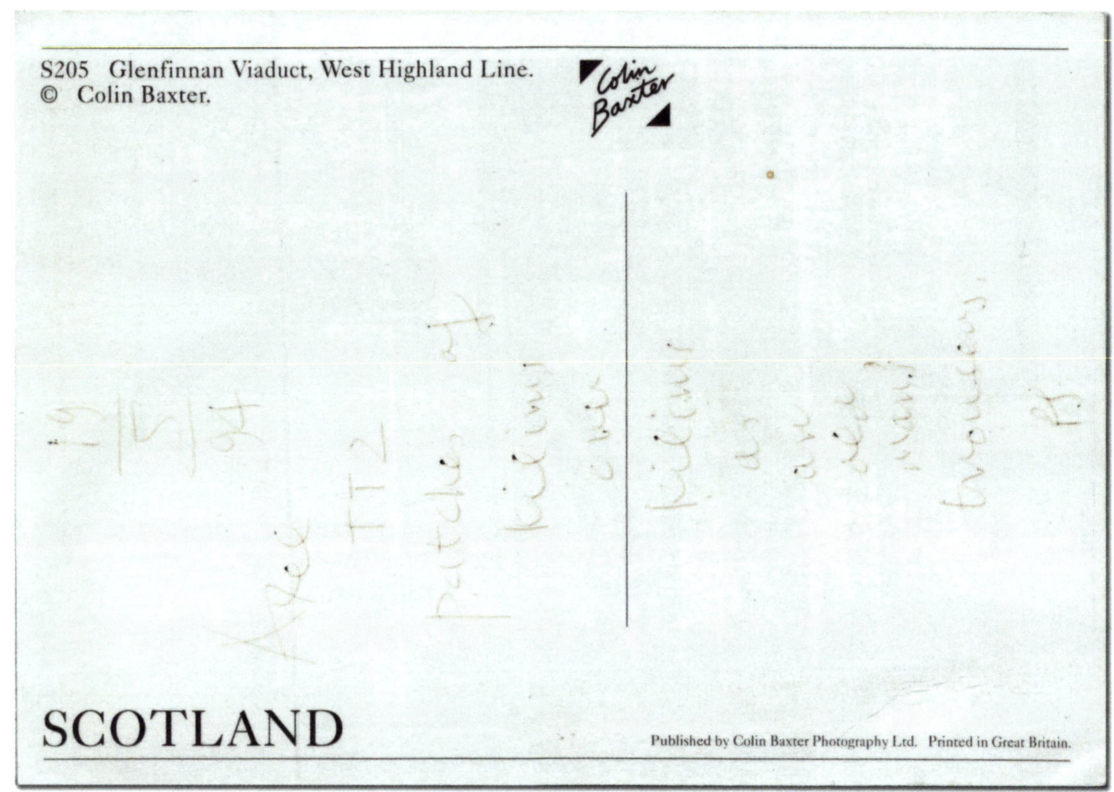

Peter Smithson, 19 May 1994

19/5/94

Axel
TT2
patches of
kilims
over
kilims
as
an
old
man's
trousers.
PS

"TT2" refers to the Trundling Turk II lounge chair, designed by Alison and Peter Smithson in 1976 and prototyped by Tecta. It was exhibited at the Cologne International Furniture Fair in 1991.

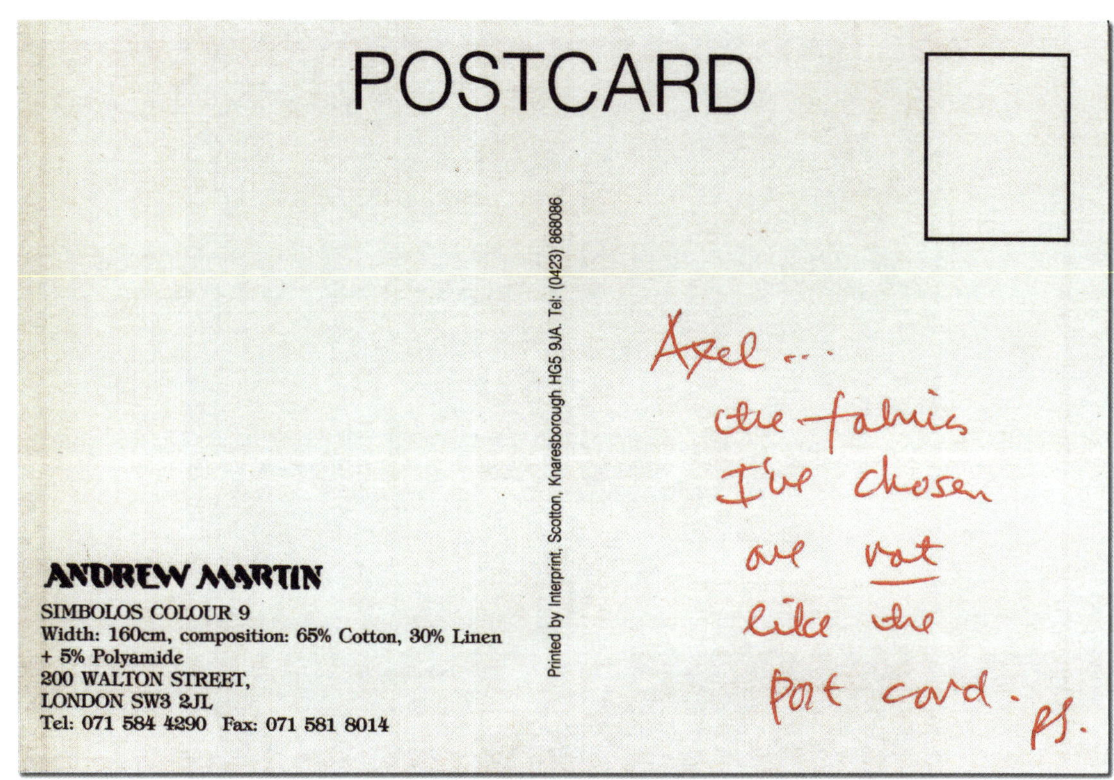
POSTCARD

Printed by Interprint, Scotton, Knaresborough HG5 9JA. Tel: (0423) 868086

ANDREW MARTIN
SIMBOLOS COLOUR 9
Width: 160cm, composition: 65% Cotton, 30% Linen
+ 5% Polyamide
200 WALTON STREET,
LONDON SW3 2JL
Tel: 071 584 4290 Fax: 071 581 8014

Axel…
the fabrics
I've chosen
are not
like the
post card. PS.

Peter Smithson, undated / circa 1994

Axel…
The fabrics
I've chosen
are <u>not</u>
like the
post card.
PS.

The postcard could be from 3 June 1994, accompanying a letter that deals with the Trundling Turk II lounge chair and its upholstery fabric. The letter mentions enclosing an Andrew Martin postcard.
Andrew Martin is a British manufacturer of designer fabrics for upholstery.

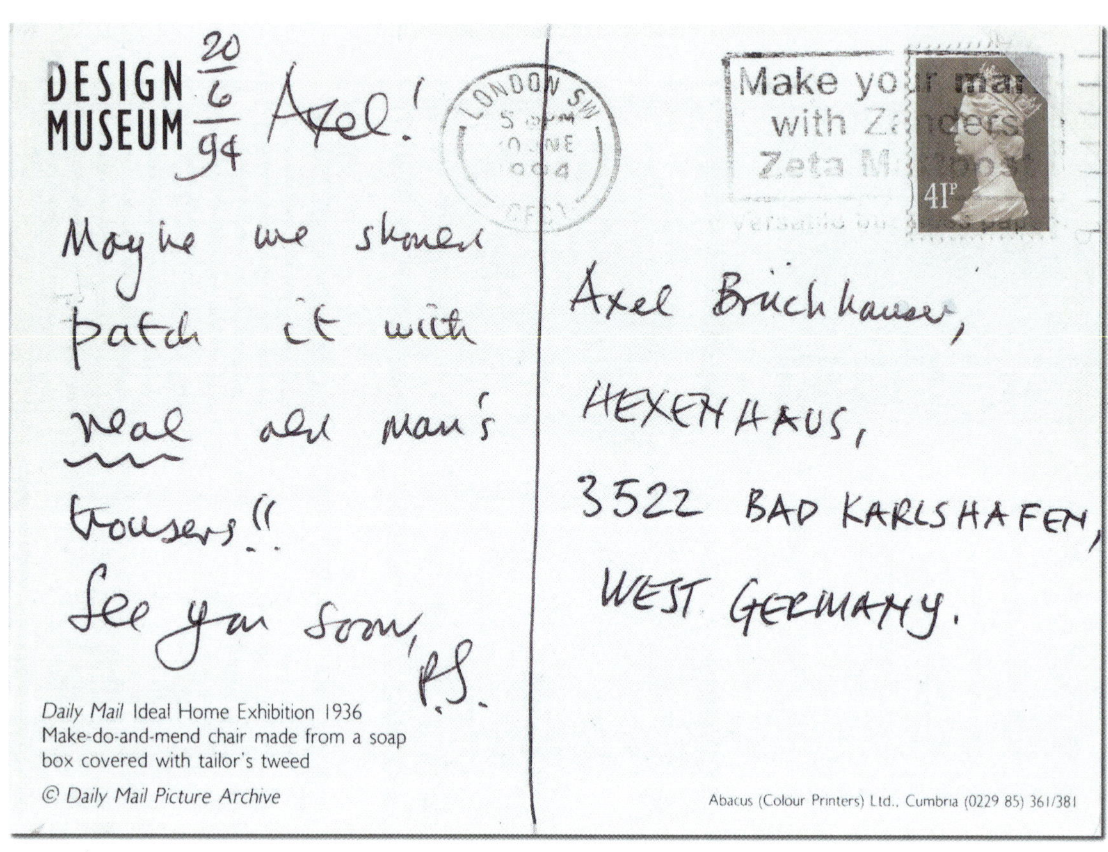

DESIGN MUSEUM
20/6/94
Axel!
Maybe we should
patch it with
real old man's
trousers!!
See you soon,
PS.
LONDON SW
Make your
with Za
Zeta M
41P
Axel Brüchhauser,
HEXENHAUS,
3522 BAD KARLSHAFEN,
WEST GERMANY.
Daily Mail Ideal Home Exhibition 1936
Make-do-and-mend chair made from a soap box covered with tailor's tweed
© Daily Mail Picture Archive
Abacus (Colour Printers) Ltd., Cumbria (0229 85) 361/381

Peter Smithson, 20 June 1994

20/6/94

Axel!
Maybe we should
patch it with
real old man's trousers!!
See you soon,
PS.

Peter and Axel were about to decide on the upholstering of the Trundling Turk II lounge chair designed by Alison and Peter Smithson. The postcard continues the conversation from the previous one.

8/9/94

Axel (via Herman Koch),

THANK-YOU FOR THE PHOTOGRAPHS.

THE STEEL IS BEAUTIFULL.

MAYBE PLAIN CUSHIONS TO LET

THE STEEL PATTERN SHOW?

(sample with Herman)

AS EVER,

P.S.

BENCH

CHAIR

Domenico Veneziano (active 1438–1461)
The Annunciation
Tempera on panel, 273 x 540 mm
FITZWILLIAM MUSEUM, CAMBRIDGE
CPC 13

Printed at The Cloister Press

Peter Smithson, 8 September 1994

8/9/94

Axel (via Herman Koch),
THANK YOU FOR THE PHOTOGRAPHS.
THE STEEL IS BEAUTIFULL.
MAYBE PLAIN CUSHIONS TO LET
THE STEEL PATTERN SHOW?
(sample with Herman)
AS EVER,
P.S.

[also written are the words “BENCH” and “CHAIR”, with arrows pointing to the two seats on the other side of the postcard]

Herman Koch, a German architect and carpenter, did an internship at the Smithsons’ office, recommended by Axel. Koch was involved in the design of the Yellow Lookout (installed in the Tecta factory courtyard in 1991) and later in the building of the Hexenbesenraum, in 1995-96.

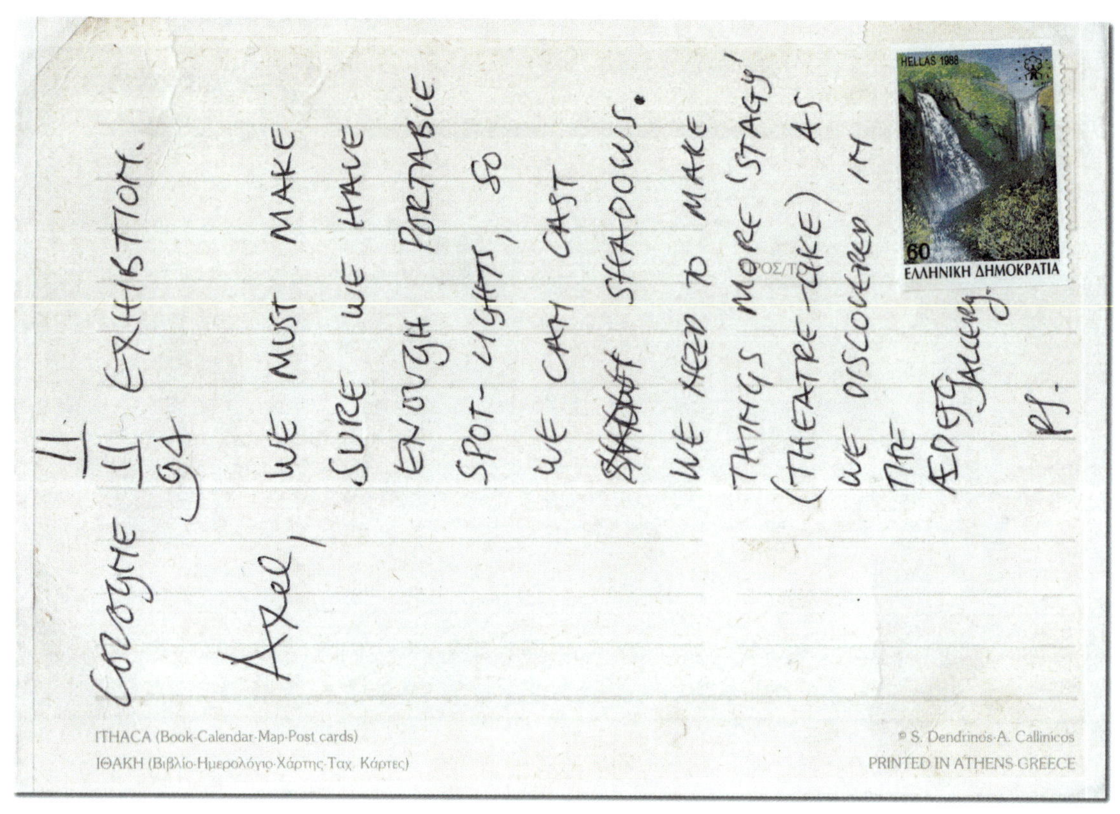

Peter Smithson, 11 November 1994

11/11/94
COLOGNE EXHIBITION

Axel, WE MUST MAKE
SURE WE HAVE
ENOUGH PORTABLE
SPOT-LIGHTS, SO
WE CAN CAST
SHADOWS.
WE NEED TO MAKE
THINGS MORE ‘STAGY’
(THEATRE-LIKE) AS
WE DISCOVERED IN THE
AEDES GALLERY.
PS.

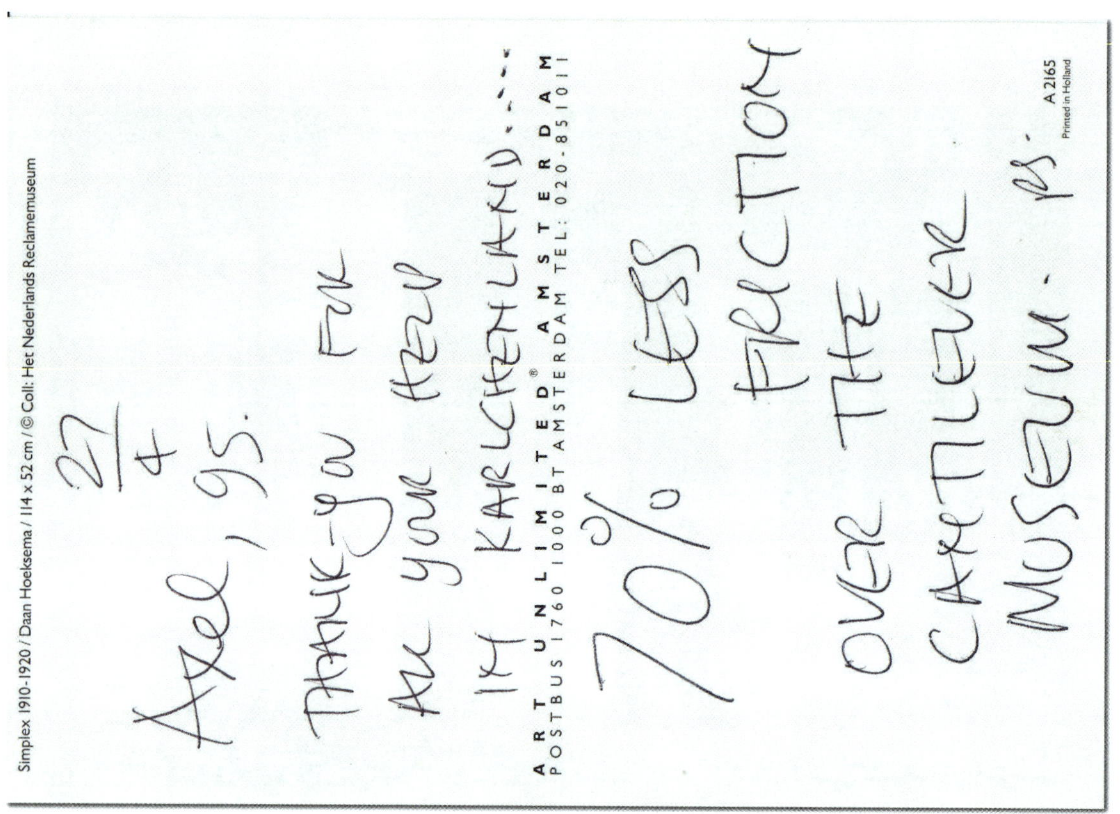

Peter Smithson, 27 April 1995

27/4/95

Axel,
THANK YOU FOR ALL YOUR HELP IN KARLCHENLAND.....
70% LESS FRICTION OVER THE CANTILEVER MUSEUM.
PS.

The Tecta Kragstuhlmuseum (i.e. the Cantilever Chair Museum) was initially established in 1983 in the town of Beverungen, within an old storage building. A dedicated museum for the Tecta chair collection was built in 2003-04 at Tecta's premises in Lauenförde, according to Peter Smithson's designs. Peter Smithson passed away shortly after handing in the construction drawings for the museum buildings.

CYCLOÏDE
70 %
LESS FRICTION
SIMPLEX
AMSTERDAM HOLLAND

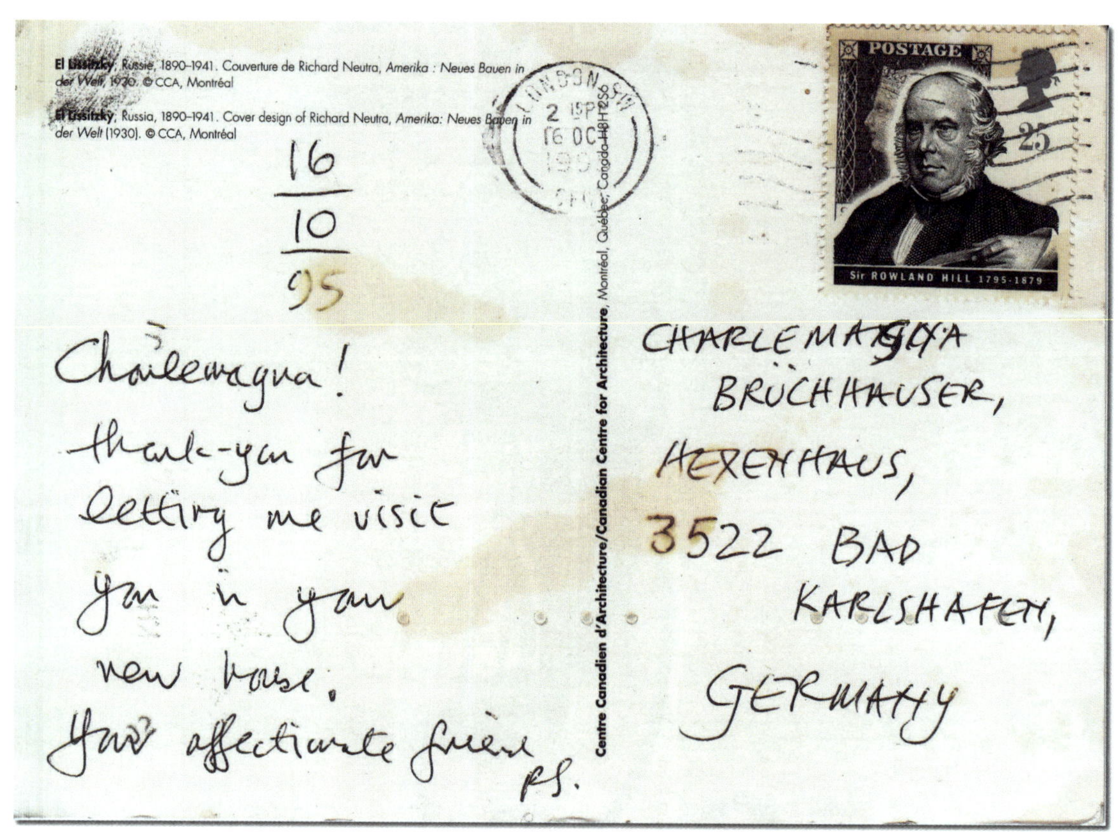

El Lissitzky, Russie, 1890–1941. Couverture de Richard Neutra, *Amerika : Neues Bauen in der Welt*, 1930. © CCA, Montréal

El Lissitzky, Russia, 1890–1941. Cover design of Richard Neutra, *Amerika: Neues Bauen in der Welt* (1930). © CCA, Montréal

Centre Canadien d'Architecture/Canadian Centre for Architecture, Montréal, Québec, Canada H3H 2S6

POSTAGE 25
Sir ROWLAND HILL 1795-1879

16/10/95

Charlemagna!
thank-you for
letting me visit
you in your
new house.
Your affectionate friend
PS.

CHARLEMAGNA
BRÜCHHAUSER,
HEXENHAUS,
3522 BAD
KARLSHAFEN,
GERMANY

Peter Smithson, 16 October 1995

16/10/95

Charlemagna!

thank-you for
letting me visit
you in your new house.
Your affectionate friend
PS.

Peter Smithson called the third Karlchen-cat Charlemagna. The postcard is addressed to this new cat, and congratulates her on her arrival to the Hexenhaus.
The ascetic marble throne of Charlemagne, King of the Franks, can be found at Aachen Cathedral. It is said that this throne was the basis of the measurements for the Barcelona Chair designed by Mies van der Rohe. A reproduction of the throne is located in the entrance to the Tecta Factory.

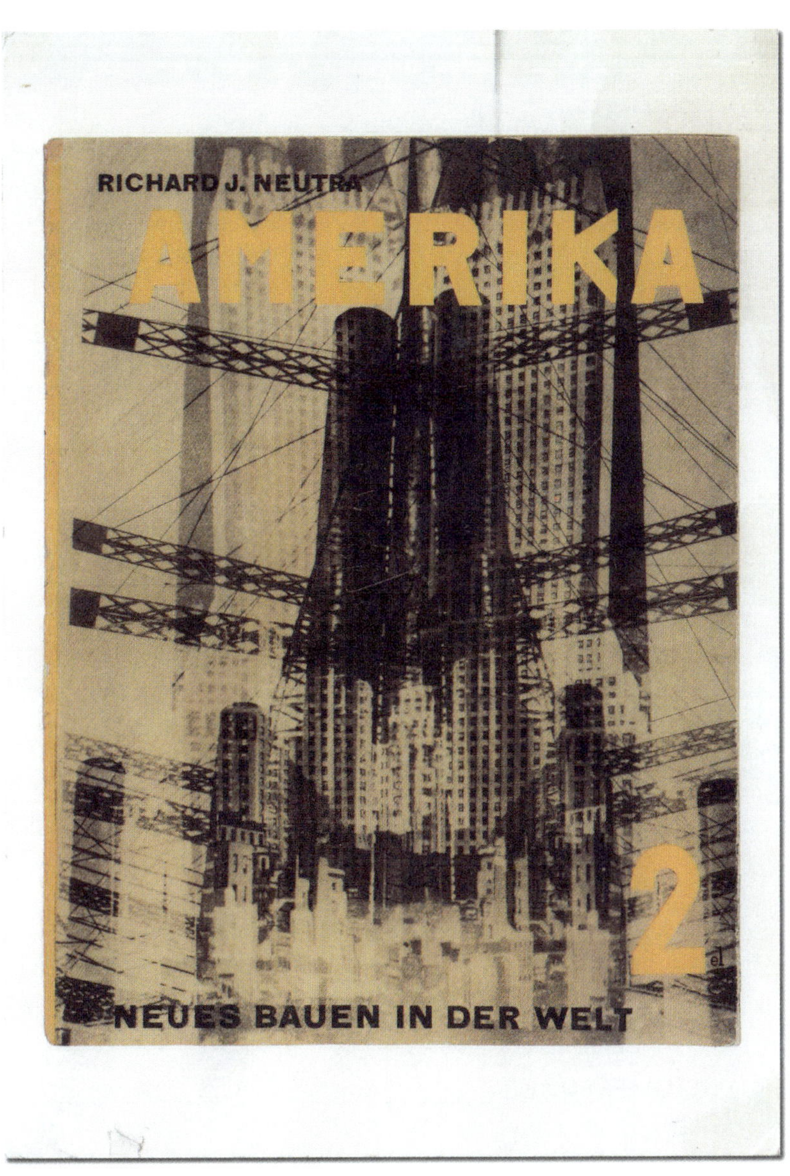
RICHARD J. NEUTRA
AMERIKA
2
NEUES BAUEN IN DER WELT

'THE THRONE
OF THE
EMPORER'

N. 492 - PINTURICCHIO
Enea Piccolomini incoronato poeta da Federico III
Aeneas Piccolomini couronné poète par Frédéric III
Aeneas Piccolomini crowned with laurel by Frederick III
Aeneas Piccolomini wird von Friedrich III. zum Dichter gekrönt
Eneas Piccolomini coronado poeta por Federico III

Libreria Piccolomini nel Duomo di Siena

Proprietà riservata

Copyright by A. Martello Editore - Milano

Printed in Italy

Peter Smithson, undated

'THE THRONE OF THE EMPORER'

Unsigned.

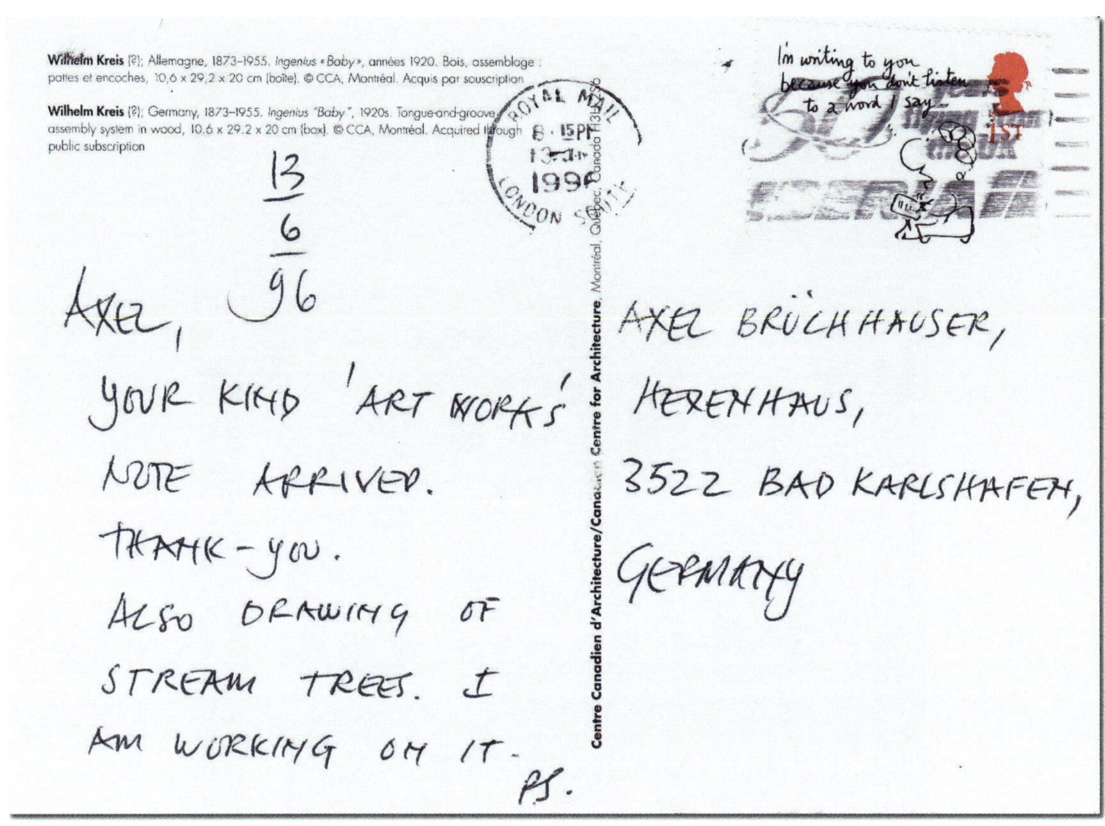
Wilhelm Kreis (?); Allemagne, 1873–1955. *Ingenius « Baby »*, années 1920. Bois, assemblage : pattes et encoches, 10,6 x 29,2 x 20 cm (boîte). © CCA, Montréal. Acquis par souscription

Wilhelm Kreis (?); Germany, 1873–1955. *Ingenius "Baby"*, 1920s. Tongue-and-groove assembly system in wood, 10.6 x 29.2 x 20 cm (box). © CCA, Montréal. Acquired through public subscription

13/6/96

AXEL,
YOUR KIND 'ART WORKS' NOTE ARRIVED.
THANK-YOU.
ALSO DRAWING OF STREAM TREES. I AM WORKING ON IT.
PS.

AXEL BRÜCHHAUSER,
HERENHAUS,
3522 BAD KARLSHAFEN,
GERMANY

Centre Canadien d'Architecture/Canadian Centre for Architecture, Montréal, Québec, Canada H3H 2S6

ROYAL MAIL
8 · 15PM
1996
LONDON
I'm writing to you because you don't listen to a word I say
1ST

Peter Smithson, 13 June 1996

13/6/96

AXEL,
YOUR KIND 'ART WORKS' NOTE ARRIVED.
THANK-YOU.
ALSO DRAWING OF STREAM TREES. I AM WORKING ON IT.
PS.

THE NEW CITY

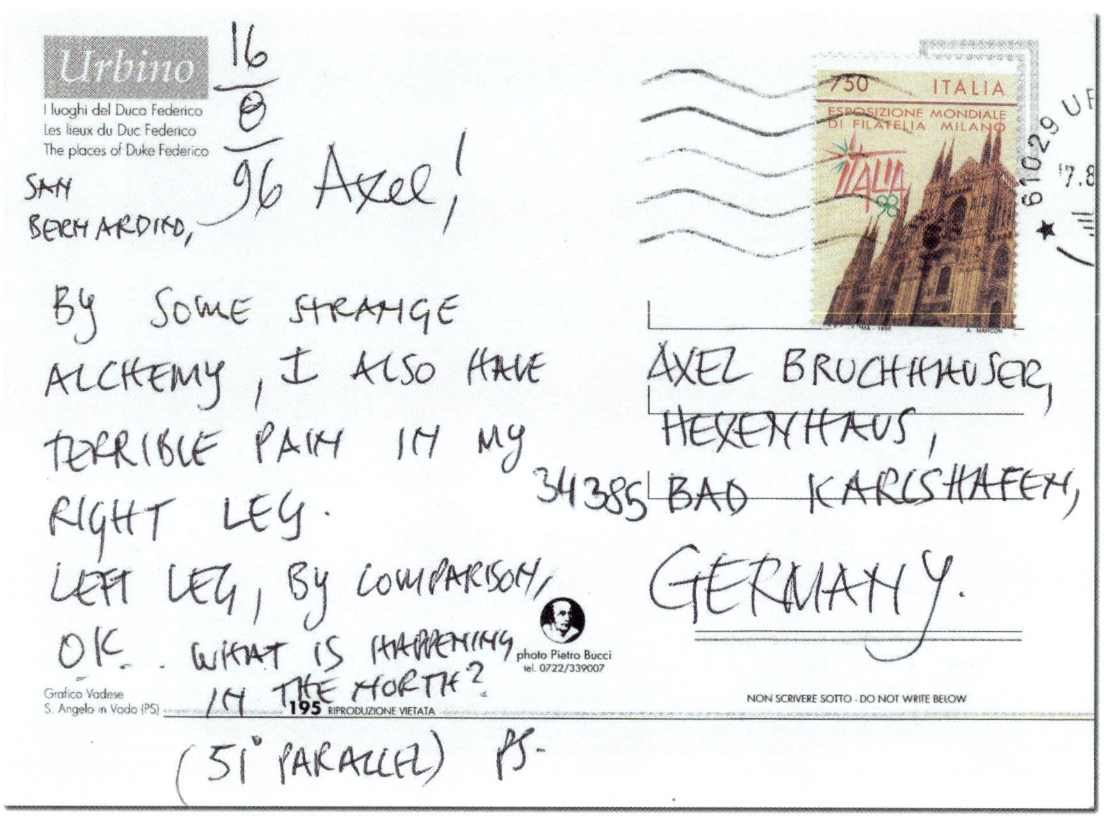

Urbino
I luoghi del Duca Federico
Les lieux du Duc Federico
The places of Duke Federico
SAN BERNARDINO, 16/8/96 Axel!
BY SOME STRANGE ALCHEMY, I ALSO HAVE TERRIBLE PAIN IN MY RIGHT LEG.
LEFT LEG, BY COMPARISON, OK. . WHAT IS HAPPENING IN THE NORTH?
(51° PARALLEL) PS.
750 ITALIA
ESPOSIZIONE MONDIALE DI FILATELIA MILANO
ITALIA 98
AXEL BRUCHHAUSER,
HEXENHAUS,
34385 BAD KARLSHAFEN,
GERMANY.
photo Pietro Bucci
tel. 0722/339007
Grafica Vadese
S. Angelo in Vado (PS)
195 RIPRODUZIONE VIETATA
NON SCRIVERE SOTTO - DO NOT WRITE BELOW

Peter Smithson, 16 August 1996

SAN BERNARDINO, 16/8/96

Axel!
BY SOME STRANGE ALCHEMY, I ALSO HAVE TERRIBLE PAIN IN MY RIGHT LEG. LEFT LEG BY COMPARISON, OK... WHAT IS HAPPENING IN THE NORTH? (51° PARALLEL) PS.

Sent from the International Laboratory for Architecture and Urban Design (ILA&UD) held in Urbino in 1996. Peter regularly participated in the ILA&UD Summer School between 1977 and 2001.

Urbino

ALISON & PETER SMITHSON CATO LODGE 24 GILSTON ROAD LONDON SW10 9SR 01-373 7423

Peter Smithson, 19 September 1996

16/9/96

Axel......
WHAT ABOUT USING THIS RED
TO MATCH THE 'RED OXIDE' OF
THE HEXEN HOUSE EXTERNAL WOODWORK.
ALISON USES A SMALL AMOUNT OF
THIS RED ON THE HEXENBESENRAUM.
[written vertically on the side]: CHECK AGAINST WOODWORK;
FABRIC WILL FADE TO MATCH?

Unsigned.

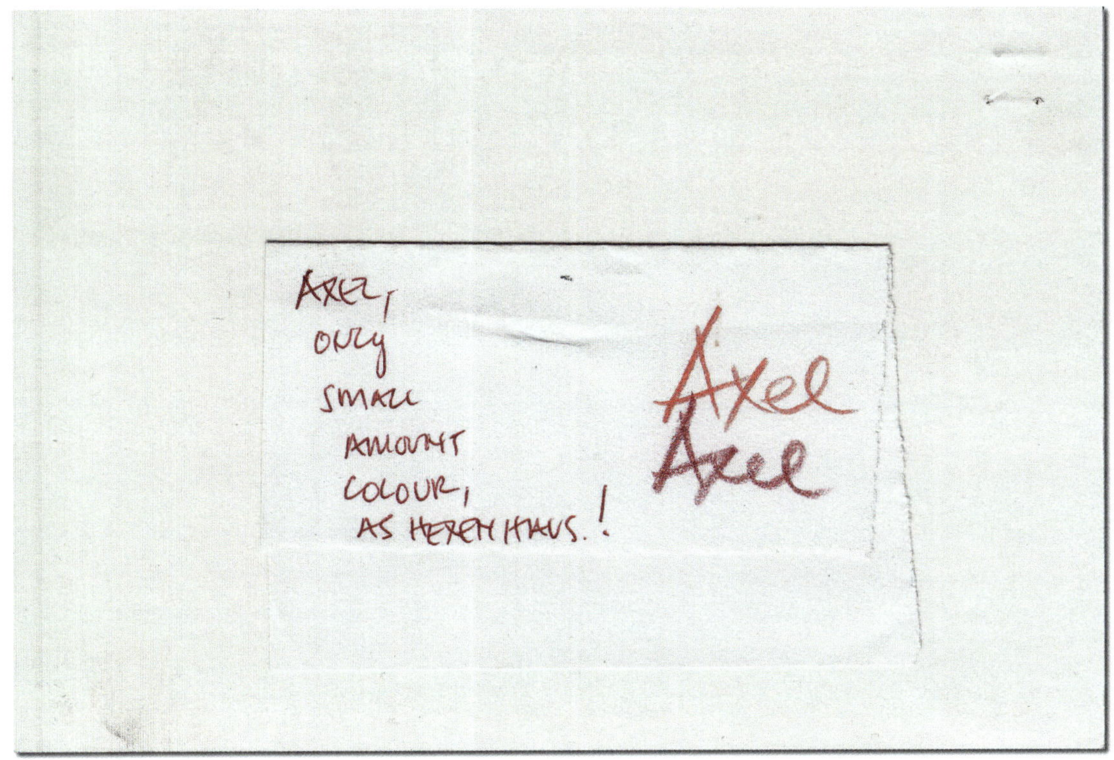

[White card with a piece of paper glued to it with the text in red]:
AXEL,
ONLY
SMALL
AMOUNT
COLOUR,
AS HEXENHAUS.!

AXEL
AXEL

The Hexenbesenraum (i.e. the "Room for the Witches' Brooms", although strictly translated Raum means "space") is a watchtower-like construction, and the first intervention at the Hexenhaus that is independent from the original building. The Hexenbesenraum was designed by Alison in 1991, but only built in 1995-96, after her death. The design was slightly modified by Peter Smithson.

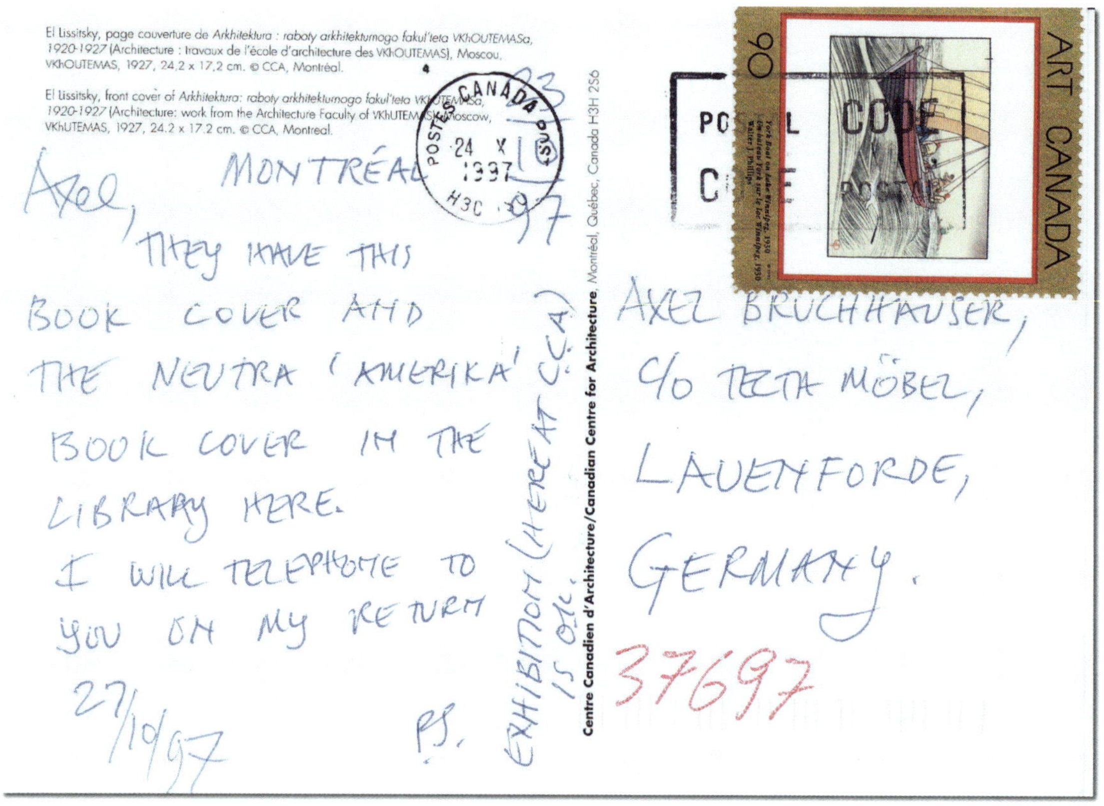

El Lissitsky, page couverture de Arkhitektura : raboty arkhitekturnogo fakul'teta VKhOUTEMASa, 1920-1927 (Architecture : travaux de l'école d'architecture des VKhOUTEMAS), Moscou, VKhOUTEMAS, 1927, 24,2 x 17,2 cm. © CCA, Montréal.
El Lissitsky, front cover of Arkhitektura: raboty arkhitekturnogo fakul'teta VKhUTEMASa, 1920-1927 (Architecture: work from the Architecture Faculty of VKhUTEMAS), Moscow, VKhUTEMAS, 1927, 24.2 x 17.2 cm. © CCA, Montreal.
Centre Canadien d'Architecture/Canadian Centre for Architecture, Montréal, Québec, Canada H3H 2S6
ART CANADA
90
POSTES CANADA
24 X 1997
Axel,
MONTRÉAL 23/10/97
THEY HAVE THIS BOOK COVER AND THE NEUTRA 'AMERIKA' BOOK COVER IN THE LIBRARY HERE.
I WILL TELEPHONE TO YOU ON MY RETURN 27/10/97
P.S.
EXHIBITION (HERE AT C.C.A.) IS OK.
AXEL BRUCHHAUSER,
C/O TECTA MÖBEL,
LAUENFORDE,
GERMANY.
37697

Peter Smithson, 23 October 1997

MONTRÉAL 23/10/97

Axel,
THEY HAVE THIS BOOK COVER AND THE NEUTRA 'AMERIKA' BOOK COVER IN THE LIBRARY HERE. I WILL TELEPHONE TO YOU ON MY RETURN 27/10/97
P.S.

[Written to the side of the postcard]: EXHIBITION (HERE AT C.C.A.) IS OK.

[Written in red pen, probably by the postal service; it corresponds to the postcode of Lauenförde]: 37697

МОСКВА
1927
АРХИТЕКТУРА
АРХИТЕКТУРА
ВХУТЕМАС
el

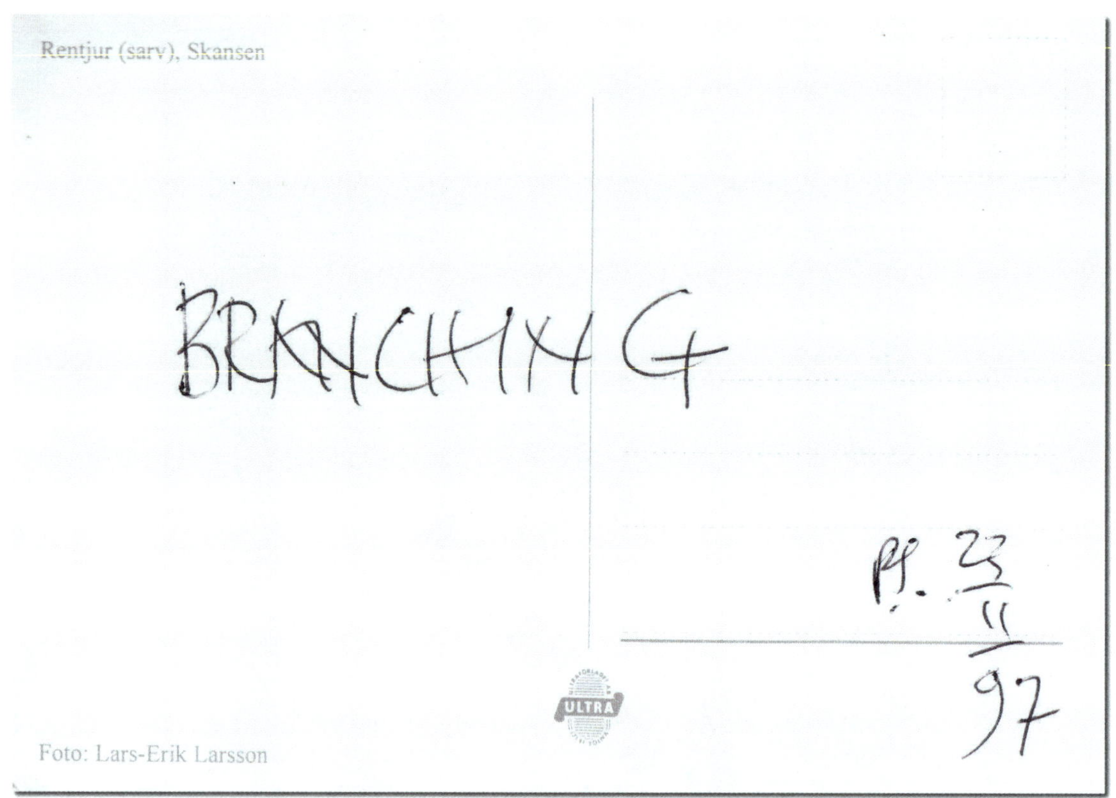

Peter Smithson, 23 November 1997

BRANCHING

PS. 23/11/97

A similar image was used as a large poster for the Lattice Furniture stand at the Cologne furniture fair in 1999. The reindeer antlers illustrate the formal solution of branching, i.e. three-dimensional lattice structures used in the Smithsons' furniture designs as well as in the Hexenhaus and Tecta interventions.

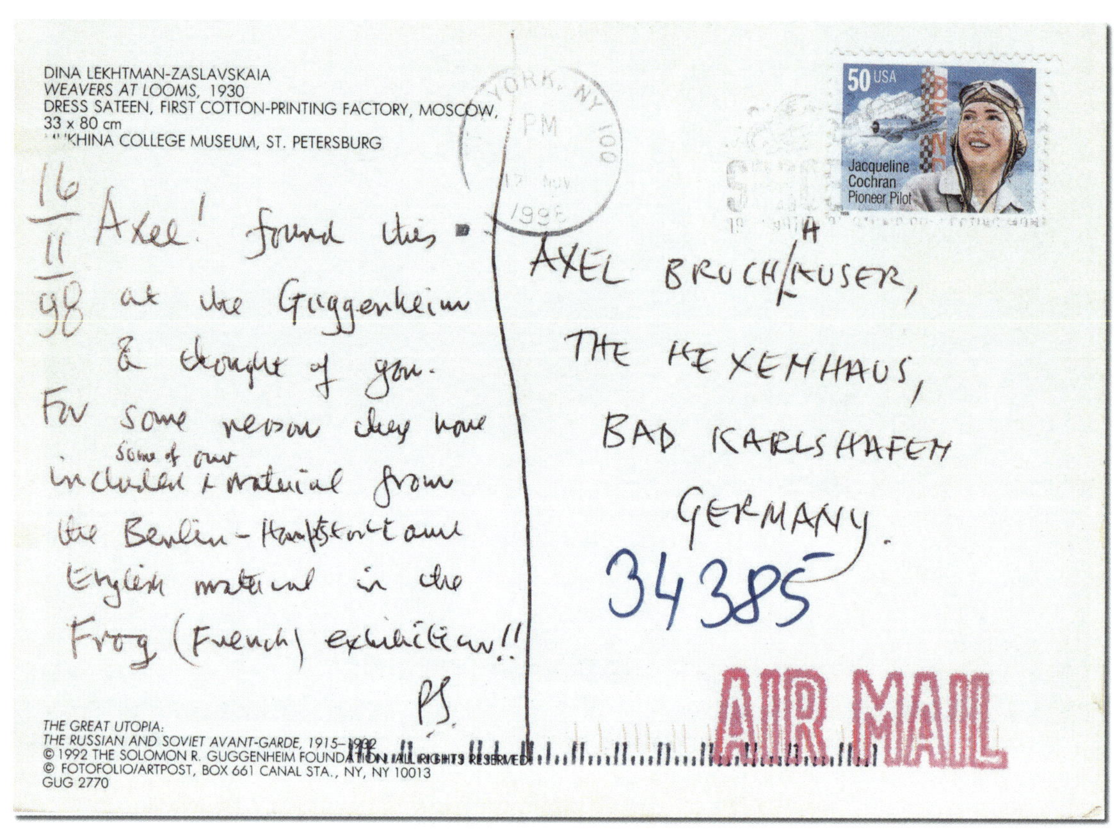
DINA LEKHTMAN-ZASLAVSKAIA
WEAVERS AT LOOMS, 1930
DRESS SATEEN, FIRST COTTON-PRINTING FACTORY, MOSCOW,
33 x 80 cm
[illegible]KHINA COLLEGE MUSEUM, ST. PETERSBURG

16/11/98 Axel! found this at the Guggenheim & thought of you. For some reason they have included some of our material from the Berlin-Hauptstadt and English material in the Frog (French) exhibition!!
PS.

AXEL BRUCHHAUSER,
THE HEXENHAUS,
BAD KARLSHAFEN
GERMANY.
34385

AIR MAIL

THE GREAT UTOPIA:
THE RUSSIAN AND SOVIET AVANT-GARDE, 1915–1932
© 1992 THE SOLOMON R. GUGGENHEIM FOUNDATION ALL RIGHTS RESERVED
© FOTOFOLIO/ARTPOST, BOX 661 CANAL STA., NY, NY 10013
GUG 2770

Peter Smithson, 16 November 1998

16/11/98

Axel! Found this at the Guggenheim & thought of you. For some reason they have included some of our material from the Berlin-Haupstadt and English material in the Frog (French) exhibition!!
P.S.

[Written in blue pen, probably by the postal service; it corresponds to the postcode of Bad Karlshafen]: 34385
Peter refers to their Berlin Haupstadt competition entry from 1957.

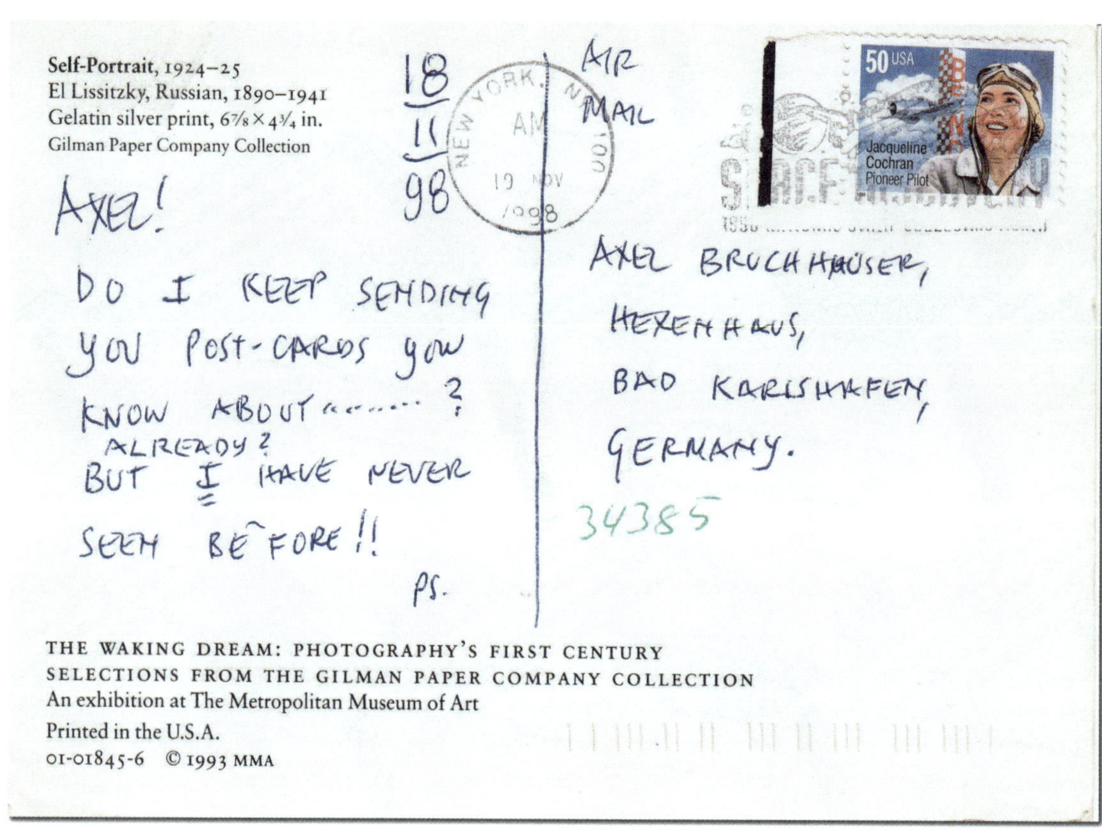
Self-Portrait, 1924–25
El Lissitzky, Russian, 1890–1941
Gelatin silver print, 6⅞ × 4¾ in.
Gilman Paper Company Collection

18
11
98

AIR
MAIL

NEW YORK, NY 100
AM
19 NOV
1998

50 USA
Jacqueline Cochran
Pioneer Pilot

AXEL!
DO I KEEP SENDING YOU POST-CARDS YOU KNOW ABOUT.......?
ALREADY?
BUT I HAVE NEVER SEEN BEFORE!!
PS.

AXEL BRUCHHAUSER,
HEXENHAUS,
BAD KARLSHAFEN,
GERMANY.

34385

THE WAKING DREAM: PHOTOGRAPHY'S FIRST CENTURY
SELECTIONS FROM THE GILMAN PAPER COMPANY COLLECTION
An exhibition at The Metropolitan Museum of Art
Printed in the U.S.A.
01-01845-6 © 1993 MMA

Peter Smithson, 18 November 1998

18/11/98

AXEL!
DO I KEEP SENDING YOU POST-CARDS YOU KNOW ABOUT.........?
ALREADY?
BUT I HAVE NEVER SEEN BEFORE!!
PS.

[Written in green pen, probably by the postal service; it corresponds to the postcode of Bad Karlshafen]: 34385

Axel is a great admirer of the kinetic art of El Lissitzky, and had studied his work in depth. As part of his research, Axel established contact with the artist's son, Jen Lissitzky, in the 1970s.

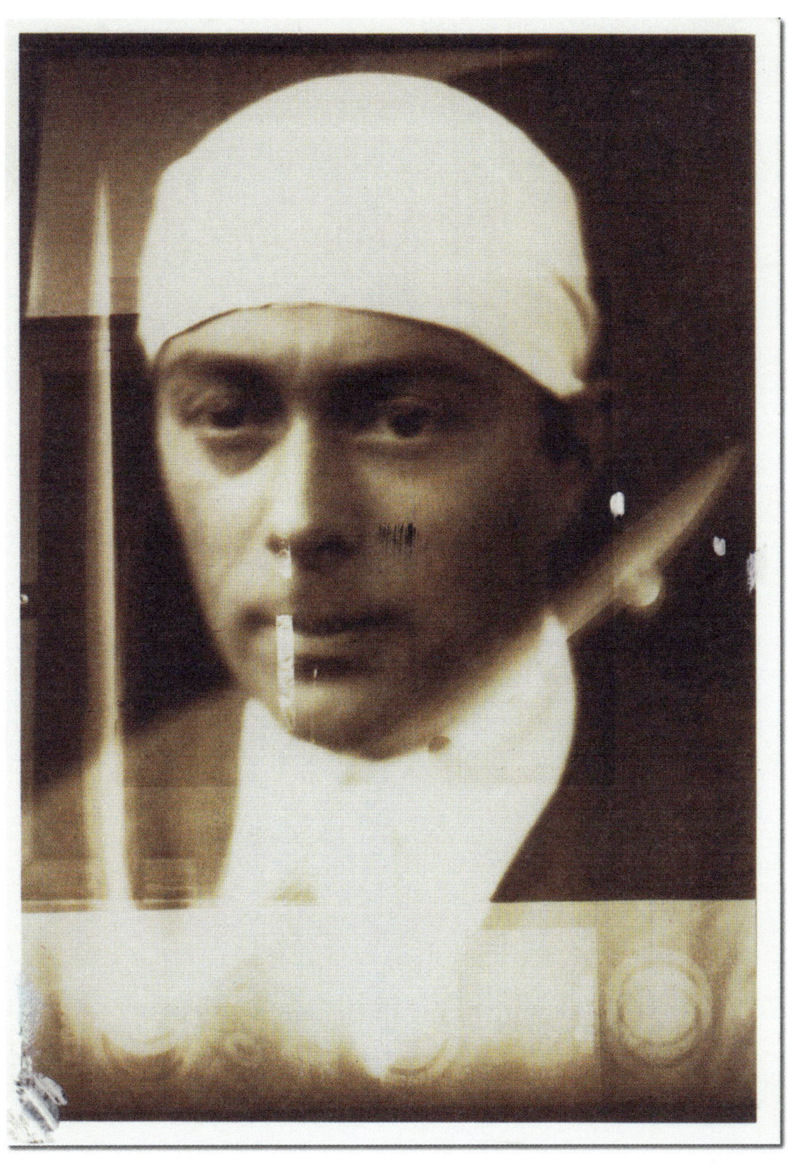

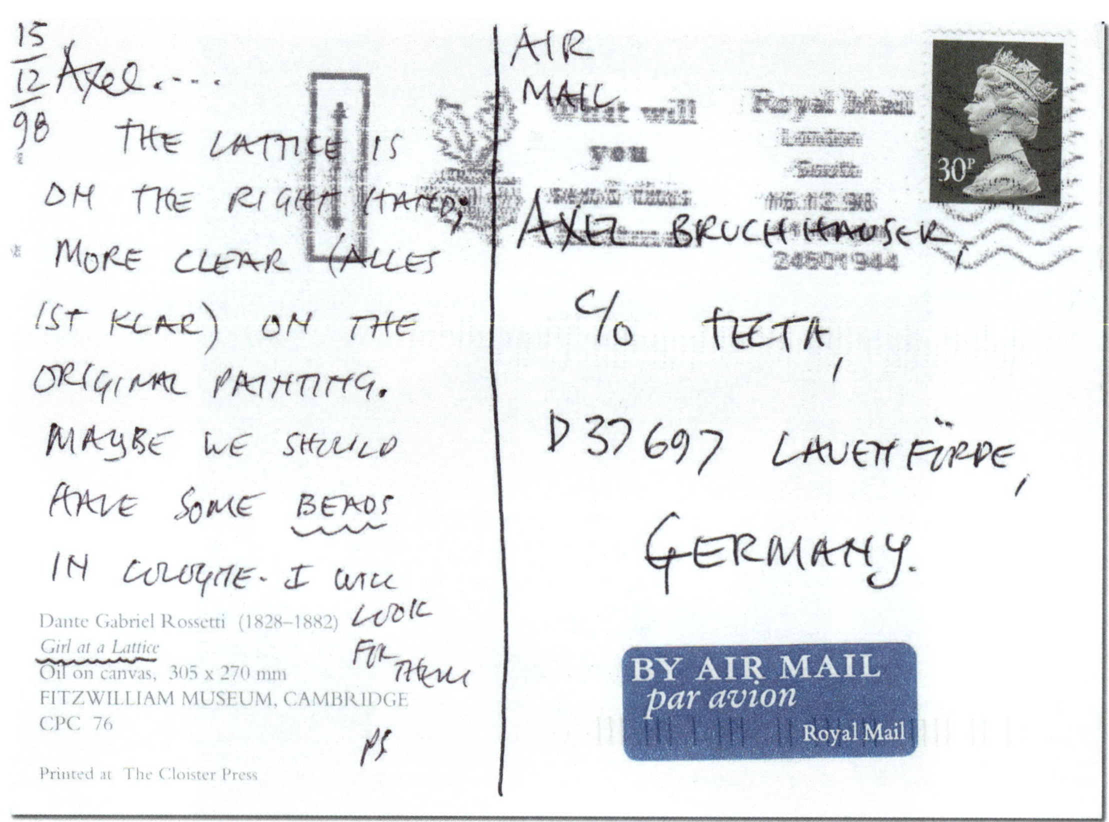
15/12/98
Axel....
THE LATTICE IS ON THE RIGHT HAND; MORE CLEAR (ALLES IST KLAR) ON THE ORIGINAL PAINTING. MAYBE WE SHOULD HAVE SOME BEADS IN COLOGNE. I WILL LOOK FOR THEM
PS

Dante Gabriel Rossetti (1828–1882)
Girl at a Lattice
Oil on canvas, 305 x 270 mm
FITZWILLIAM MUSEUM, CAMBRIDGE
CPC 76
Printed at The Cloister Press

AIR MAIL
AXEL BRUCHHAUSER,
c/o TECTA,
D 37697 LAUENFÖRDE,
GERMANY.

30P
Royal Mail London South 15.12.98
BY AIR MAIL
par avion
Royal Mail

Peter Smithson, 15 December 1998

15/12/98

Axel....
THE LATTICE IS ON THE RIGHT HAND; MORE CLEAR (ALLES IST KLAR) ON THE ORIGINAL PAINTING. MAYBE WE SHOULD HAVE SOME BEADS IN COLOGNE. I WILL LOOK FOR THEM
PS

Peter refers to the *On the Floor Off the Floor* exhibition at the Mautsch Gallery (Cologne) in 1998, where the Smithsons' lattice furniture was showcased. Furthermore, the title of the work depicted on the postcard, *Girl at a Lattice*, has been underlined.

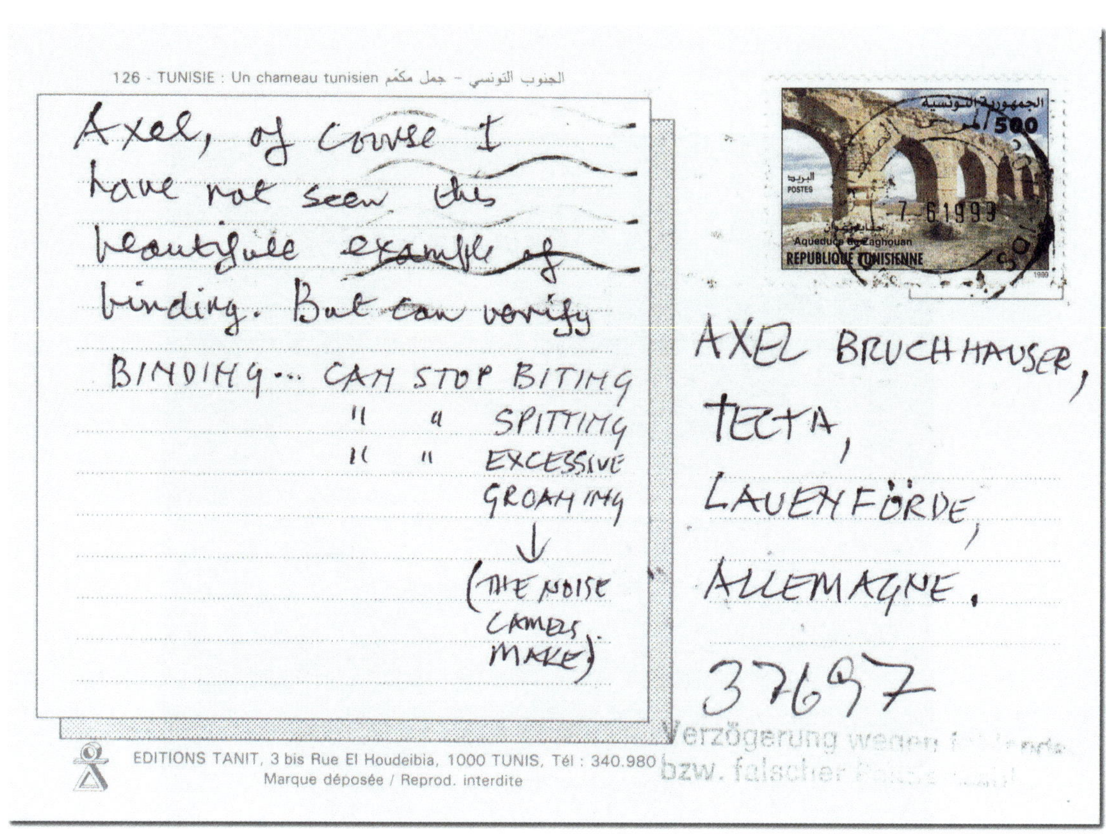

126 - TUNISIE : Un chameau tunisien جمل مكمم - الجنوب التونسي
Axel, of course I have not seen this beautifull example of binding. But can verify
BINDING... CAN STOP BITING
" " SPITTING
" " EXCESSIVE GROANING
(THE NOISE CAMELS MAKE)
Aqueduc de Zaghouan
REPUBLIQUE TUNISIENNE
500
POSTES
AXEL BRUCHHAUSER,
TECTA,
LAUENFÖRDE,
ALLEMAGNE.
37697
EDITIONS TANIT, 3 bis Rue El Houdeibia, 1000 TUNIS, Tél : 340.980
Marque déposée / Reprod. interdite

Peter Smithson, 7 June 1999

Axel, of course I have not seen this beautifull example of binding. But can verify
BINDING... CAN STOP BITING
" " SPITTING
" " EXCESSIVE GROANING
↓
(THE NOISE CAMELS MAKE)

Unsigned.

TUNISIE

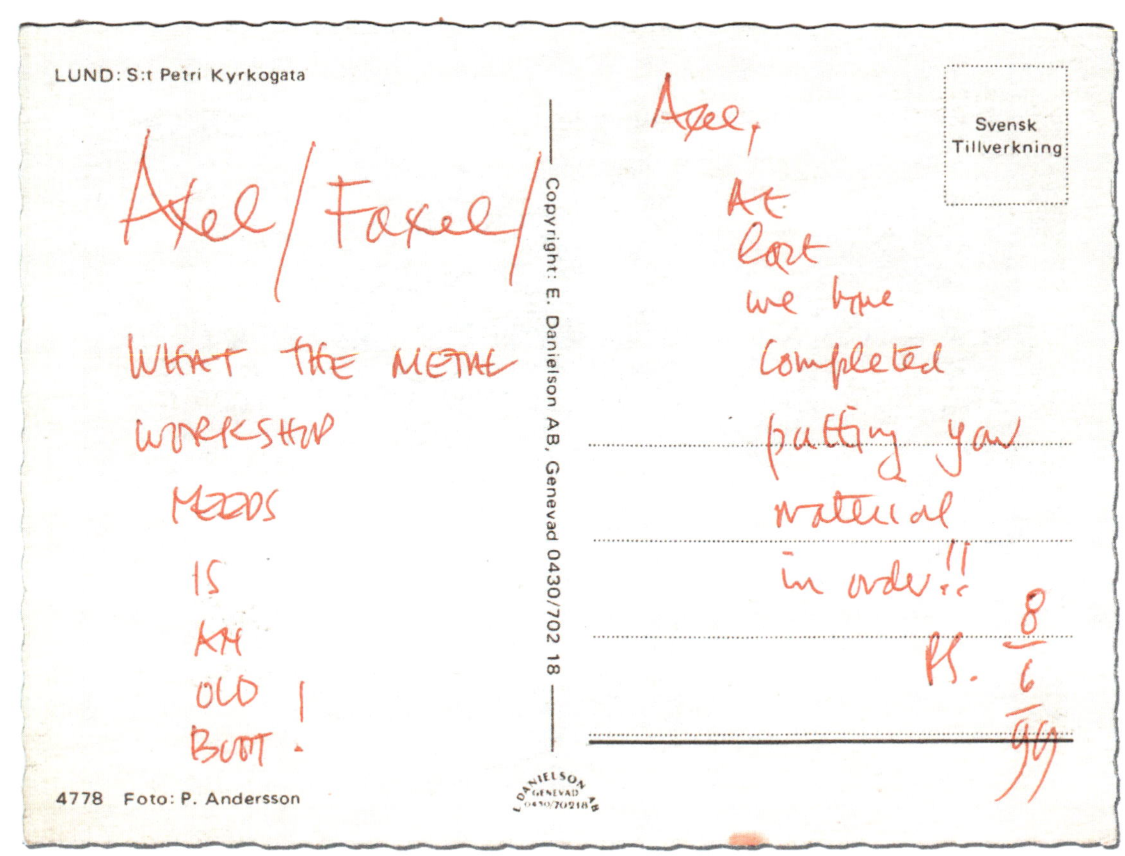

Peter Smithson, 8 June 1999

Axel / Faxel /

WHAT THE METAL
WORKSHOP
NEEDS
IS
AN
OLD
BOOT!

[Text written in the address section of the postcard]:
Axel,
At last we have completed putting your material in order!!
PS.
8/6/99

The Tecta metal workshop has a porch added by Peter Smithson in 1998-99.

FRISÖR
Lilla Boden

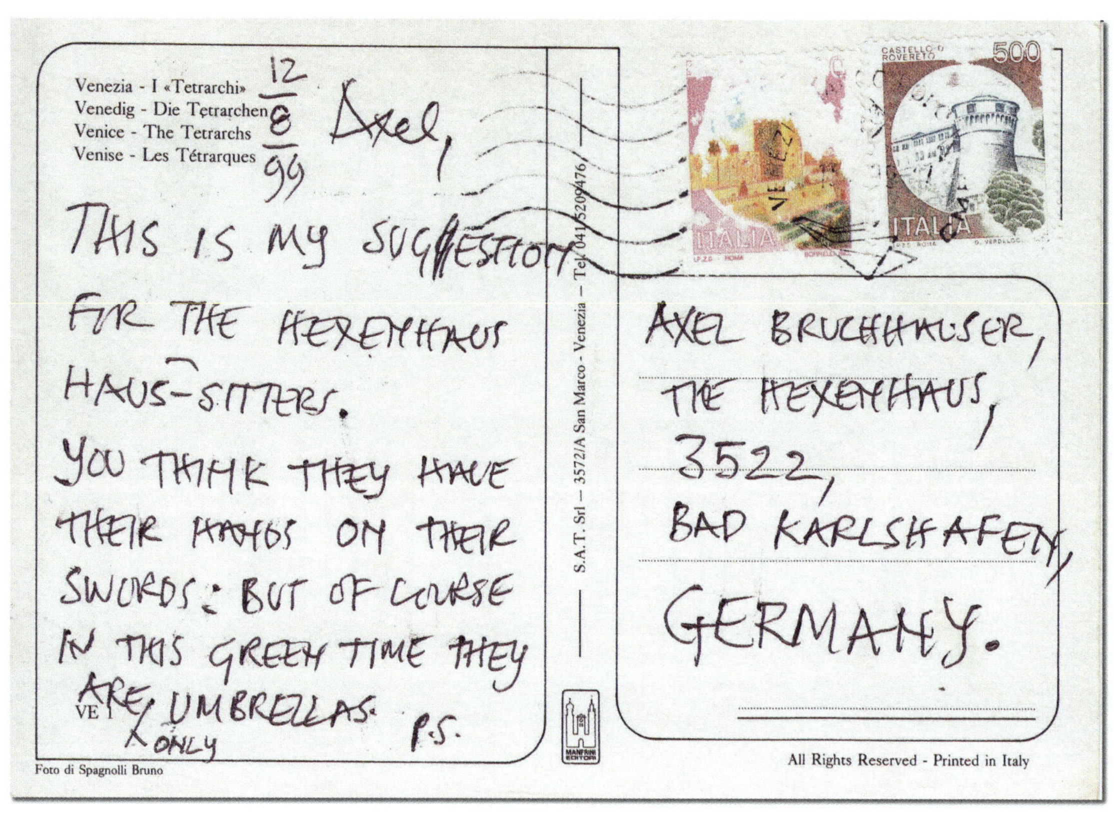
Venezia - I «Tetrarchi»
Venedig - Die Tetrarchen
Venice - The Tetrarchs
Venise - Les Tétrarques

12/8/99

Axel,
THIS IS MY SUGGESTION FOR THE HEXENHAUS HAUS-SITTERS. YOU THINK THEY HAVE THEIR HANDS ON THEIR SWORDS: BUT OF COURSE IN THIS GREEN TIME THEY ARE ONLY UMBRELLAS.
P.S.

S.A.T. Srl – 3572/A San Marco - Venezia – Tel. 041/5209476

AXEL BRUCHHAUSER,
THE HEXENHAUS,
3522,
BAD KARLSHAFEN,
GERMANY.

Foto di Spagnolli Bruno

All Rights Reserved - Printed in Italy

Peter Smithson, 12 August 1999

12/8/99

Axel,
THIS IS MY SUGGESTION FOR THE HEXENHAUS HAUS-SITTERS. YOU THINK THEY HAVE THEIR HANDS ON THEIR SWORDS: BUT OF COURSE IN THIS GREEN TIME THEY ARE ONLY UMBRELLAS.
P.S.

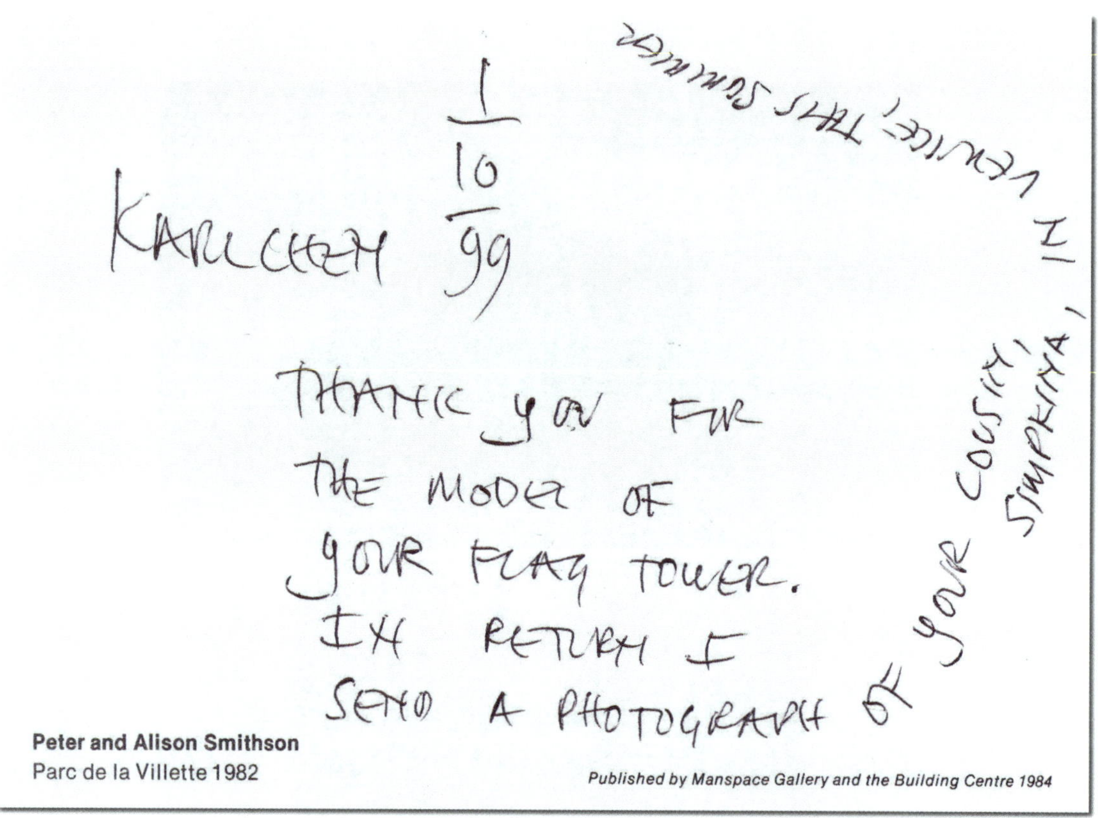
KARLCHEN 1/10/99

THANK YOU FOR THE MODEL OF YOUR FLAG TOWER. IN RETURN I SEND A PHOTOGRAPH OF YOUR COUSIN, SIMPKINA, IN VENICE, THIS SUMMER

Peter and Alison Smithson
Parc de la Villette 1982

Published by Manspace Gallery and the Building Centre 1984

Peter Smithson, 1 October 1999

1/10/99
KARLCHEN

THANK YOU FOR THE MODEL OF YOUR FLAG TOWER.
IN RETURN I SEND A PHOTOGRAPH OF YOUR COUSIN, SIMPKINA, IN VENICE, THIS SUMMER

Unsigned.

[Text below the image]: Cow pasture with a bronze herd of Charolais standing in lush looking meadow grass in which buttercups are allowed to grow before the first cut. Beech hedges contain purple sycamores; the free-standing specimen trees are willows (set against hornbeam hedges) and copper beeches. To the east the pyrocanthus clothed cone that conceals the globe; its facetted top contains observatories for armatures.
AMS February 2/81

Addressed to Karlchen the cat, and referring to the design of Karlchen's Flag Tower. Herman Koch, a German architect and wood joiner who had interned at the Smithsons' office, made a model of the tower.

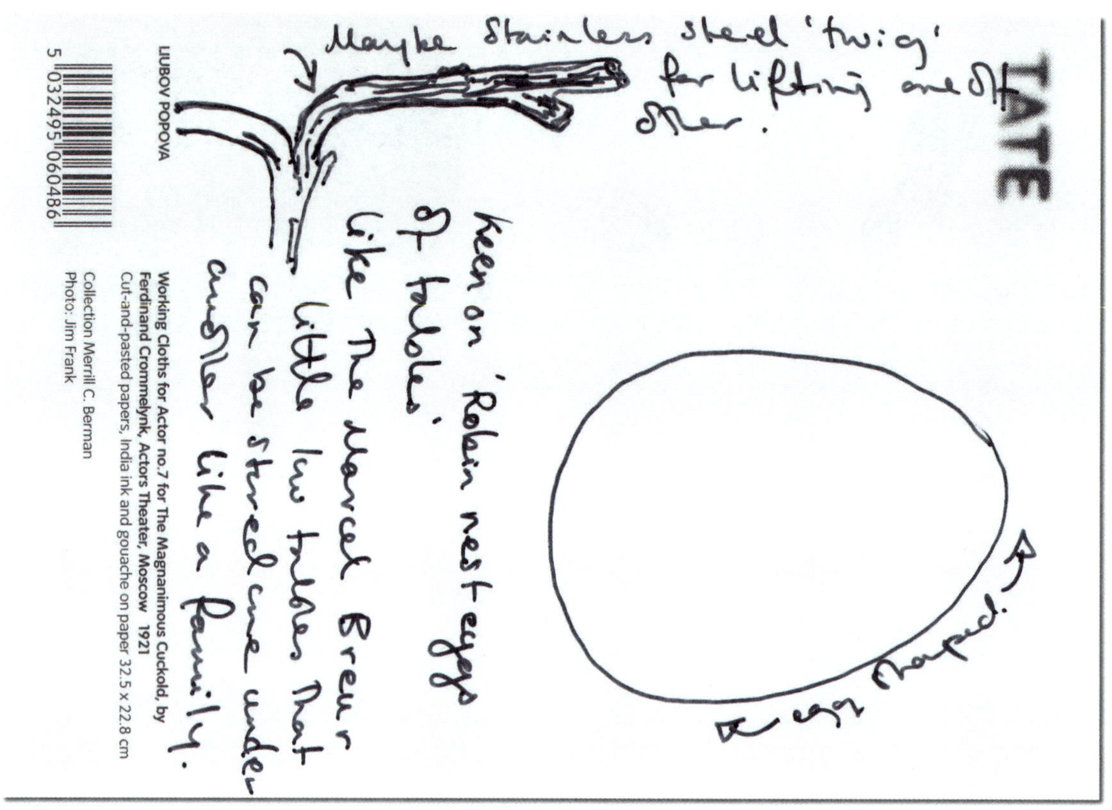

Peter Smithson, undated / circa 2000

[A sketch of an egg with a note on its side and arrows pointing in both directions]: egg shaped.

Keen on 'Robin nest eggs of tables' like the Marcel Breur little low tables that can be stored one under another like a family.

[A sketch of a branch opening in two directions, with a note on its side and an arrow pointing to the drawing]: Maybe stainless steel 'twig' for lifting one off other.

Unsigned.

The Liubov Popova image on the postcard was used to explain the colour scheme of the Popova Lattice Chair designed by Peter in 1999. In the end, the branching egg table was produced in circular form. This postcard is probably from around the year 2000: it features the new Tate logo, which was unveiled that year.

ПРОЗОДЕЖДА
АКТЕРА
№ 7
Л. ПОПОВА. 1921.

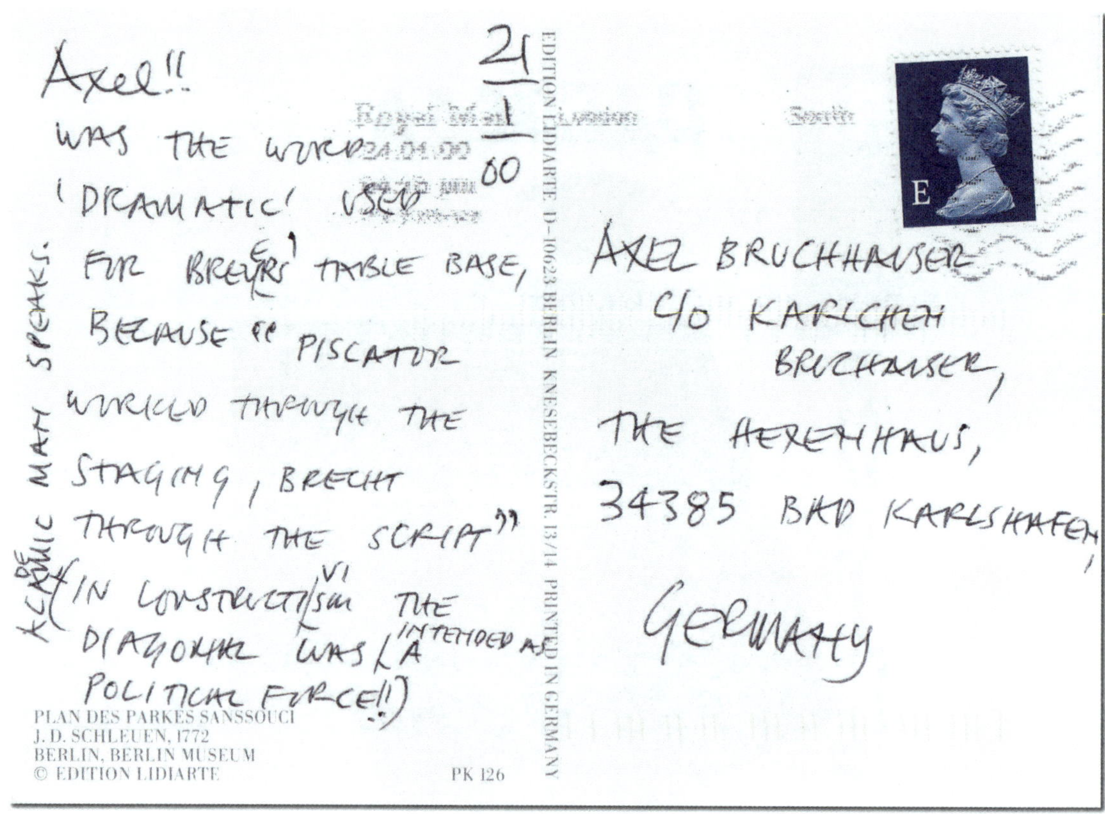

Peter Smithson, 21 January 2000

21/1/00

Axel!!
WAS THE WORD 'DRAMATIC' USED FOR BREUER'S TABLE BASE, BECAUSE "PISCATOR WORKED THROUGH THE STAGING, BRECHT THROUGH THE SCRIPT"
(IN CONSTRUCTIVISM THE DIAGONAL WAS INTENDED AS A POLITICAL FORCE!!)
[Written on the side of the postcard]: ACADEMIC MAN SPEAKS.

Unsigned.

DER PARK VON SANSSOUCI BEI POTSDAM

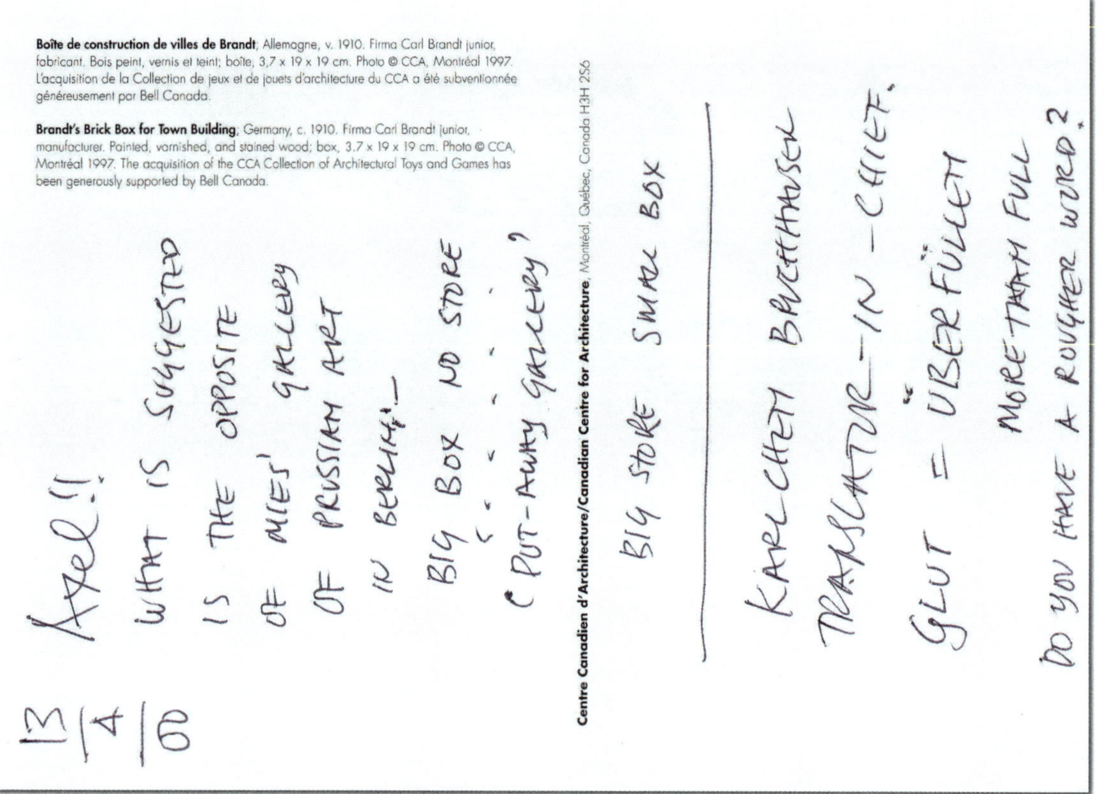

Peter Smithson, 13 April 2000

13/4/00

AXEL!
WHAT IS SUGGESTED IS THE OPPOSITE OF MIES' GALLERY OF PRUSSIAN ART
IN BERLIN; - BIG BOX NO STORE ..... 'PUT-AWAY GALLERY'
BIG STORE SMALL BOX

[Text written in the address section of the postcard]:
KARLCHEN BRUCHHAUSER
TRANSLATOR-IN-CHIEF.
GLUT = ÜBERFÜLLEN
MORE THAN FULL
DO YOU HAVE A ROUGHER WORD?

Unsigned.

See: Smithson, Peter, "Response to the Glut", in Risselada, Max and Van den Heuvel, Dirk (eds.), *Alison and Peter Smithson: From the House of the Future to the House of Today*, Rotterdam: 010 Publishers, 2004, pp. 219-220.

N. 253a.
Brandt's Städte-Baukasten.
Boîte de construction de villes (de Brandt).
Brandt's Brick Box for Town building.
Modèle déposé.
Gesetzlich geschützt.
Registered.

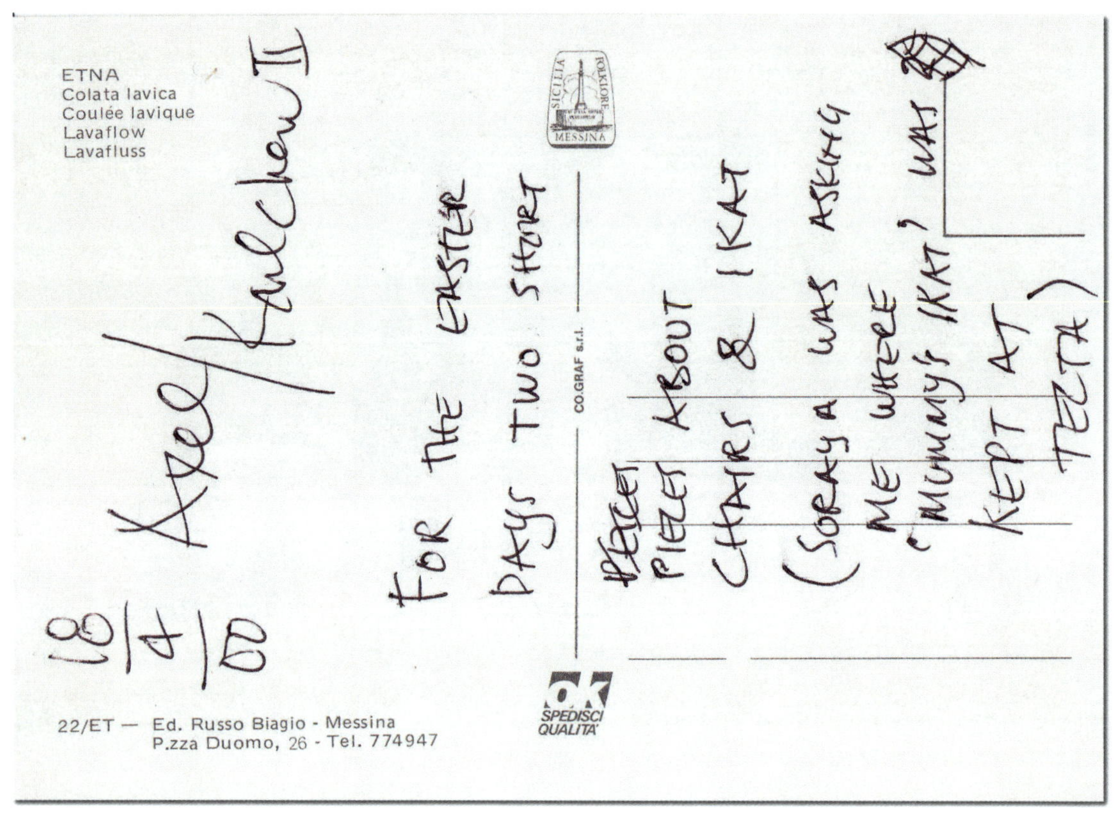

ETNA
Colata lavica
Coulée lavique
Lavaflow
Lavafluss
SICILIA FOLKLORE
MESSINA
CO.GRAF s.r.l.
OK
SPEDISCI
QUALITA'
22/ET — Ed. Russo Biagio - Messina
P.zza Duomo, 26 - Tel. 774947

Peter Smithson, 18 April 2000

18/4/00

Axel / Karlchen II
FOR THE EASTER DAYS TWO SHORT PIECES ABOUT CHAIRS & IKAT
(SORAYA WAS ASKING ME WHERE 'MUMMY'S IKAT' WAS KEPT AT TECTA)

Unsigned.

Artist Soraya Smithson is the youngest daughter of Alison and Peter Smithson.

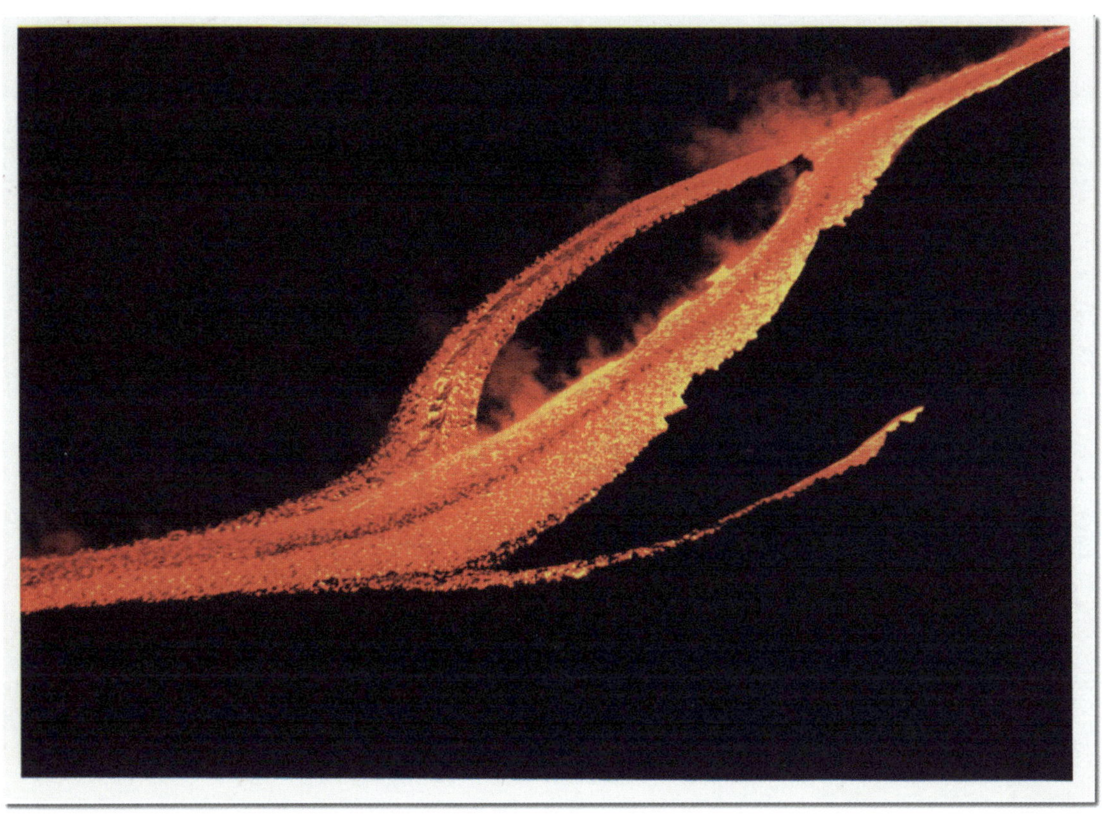

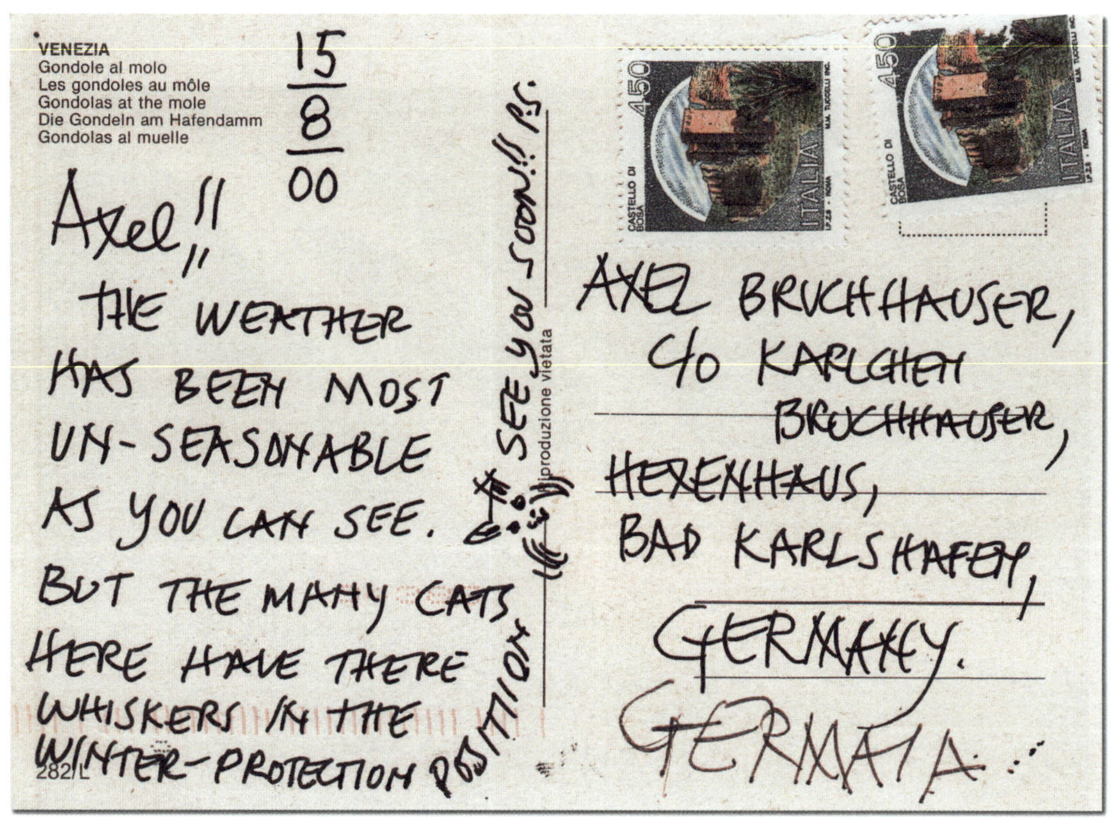
VENEZIA
Gondole al molo
Les gondoles au môle
Gondolas at the mole
Die Gondeln am Hafendamm
Gondolas al muelle

15/8/00

Axel!!
THE WEATHER
HAS BEEN MOST
UN-SEASONABLE
AS YOU CAN SEE.
BUT THE MANY CATS
HERE HAVE THERE
WHISKERS IN THE
WINTER-PROTECTION POSITION

SEE YOU SOON!! P.S.

riproduzione vietata

282/L

ITALIA 450 CASTELLO DI BOSA

AXEL BRUCHHAUSER,
C/O KARLCHEN
BRUCHHAUSER,
HEXENHAUS,
BAD KARLSHAFEN,
GERMANY.
GERMANIA

Peter Smithson, 15 August 2000

15/8/00

Axel!!
THE WEATHER
HAS BEEN MOST
UN-SEASONABLE
AS YOU CAN SEE.
BUT THE MANY CATS
HERE HAVE THERE
WHISKERS IN THE
WINTER-PROTECTION POSITION [a drawing of a cat with the whiskers pointing downwards]
SEE YOU SOON!! P.S.

Sent from the International Laboratory for Architecture and Urban Design (ILA&UD) held in Venice in 2000. Peter regularly participated in the ILA&UD Summer School between 1977 and 2001.

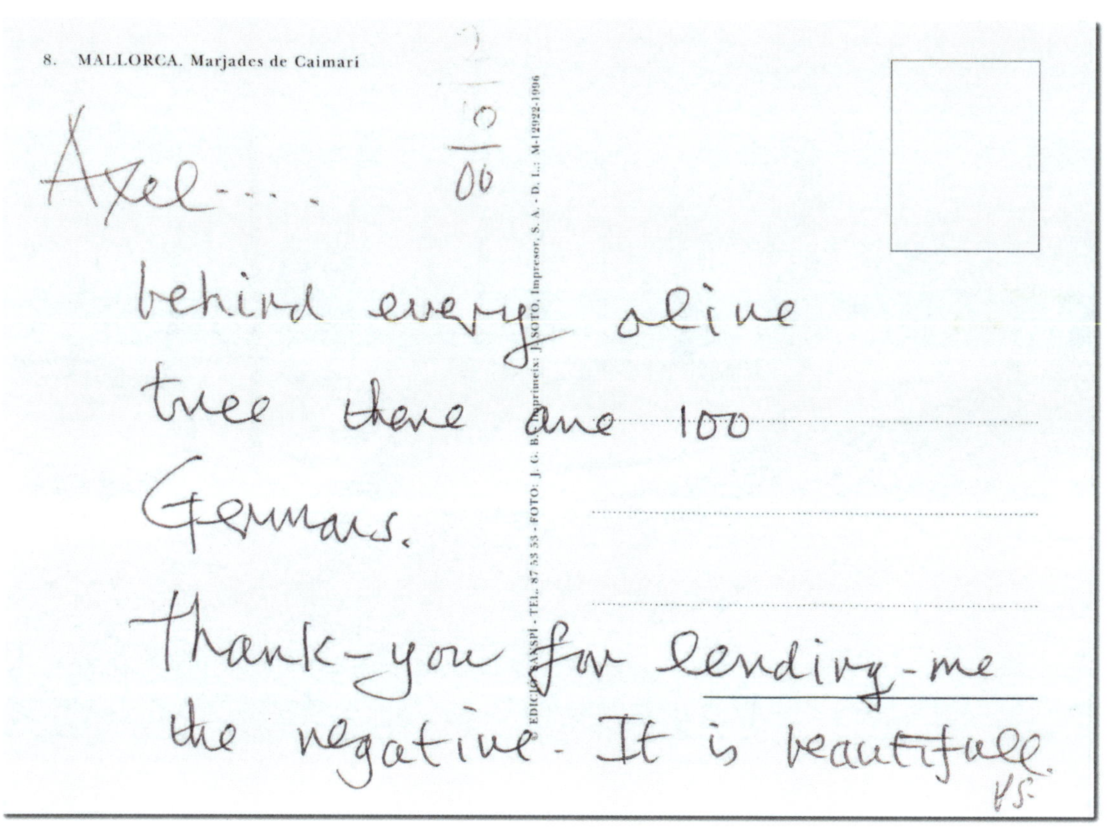

Peter Smithson, 2 October 2000

2/10/00

Axel....
Behind every olive tree there are 100 Germans.
Thank-you for lending me the negative. It is beautifull.
PS.

Sent while Peter was visiting the workshop organised by the Spanish architect Carme Pinós in Mallorca.

JEAN DUBUFFET (Le Havre,*1901)
Coucou Bazar, 1973
Musée Guggenheim, New York et Grand Palais, Paris (1973)
Promotrice delle Belle Arti al Valentino, Turin (1978)
Fondation Jean Dubuffet, Périgny-sur-Yerres, (Val de Marne)

VD 721 - Kunstkartendruck Vontobel, Feldmeilen/Zürich - Printed in Switzerland
© 1980, Copyright by ADAGP, Paris and COSMOPRESS, Geneva

Axel!
ANOTHER USE
FOR LANTERN
PAVILION!
'ACTORS' INSIDE
AUDIENCE OUTSIDE
(WITH MICROPHONES INSIDE)
SITTING ON BANK
ABOVE

Peter Smithson, undated / circa 2000-01

Axel!
ANOTHER USE FOR LANTERN PAVILION!
'ACTORS' INSIDE
AUDIENCE OUTSIDE
(WITH MICROPHONES INSIDE)
SITTING ON BANK
ABOVE

Unsigned.

The Lantern Pavilion was designed and built between 2000 and 2001. The postcard could be from then.
Most of the Hexenhaus interventions connect the house to its surrounding nature, either visually (porches, windows, holes) or physically (bridges and piers). The Lantern Pavilion, a late addition to the Hexenhaus constellation, did not solve a detected problem or address a particular need, but rather was a whim of the architect and his client. Peter proposed several imaginative functions for the "useless" Lantern Pavilion.

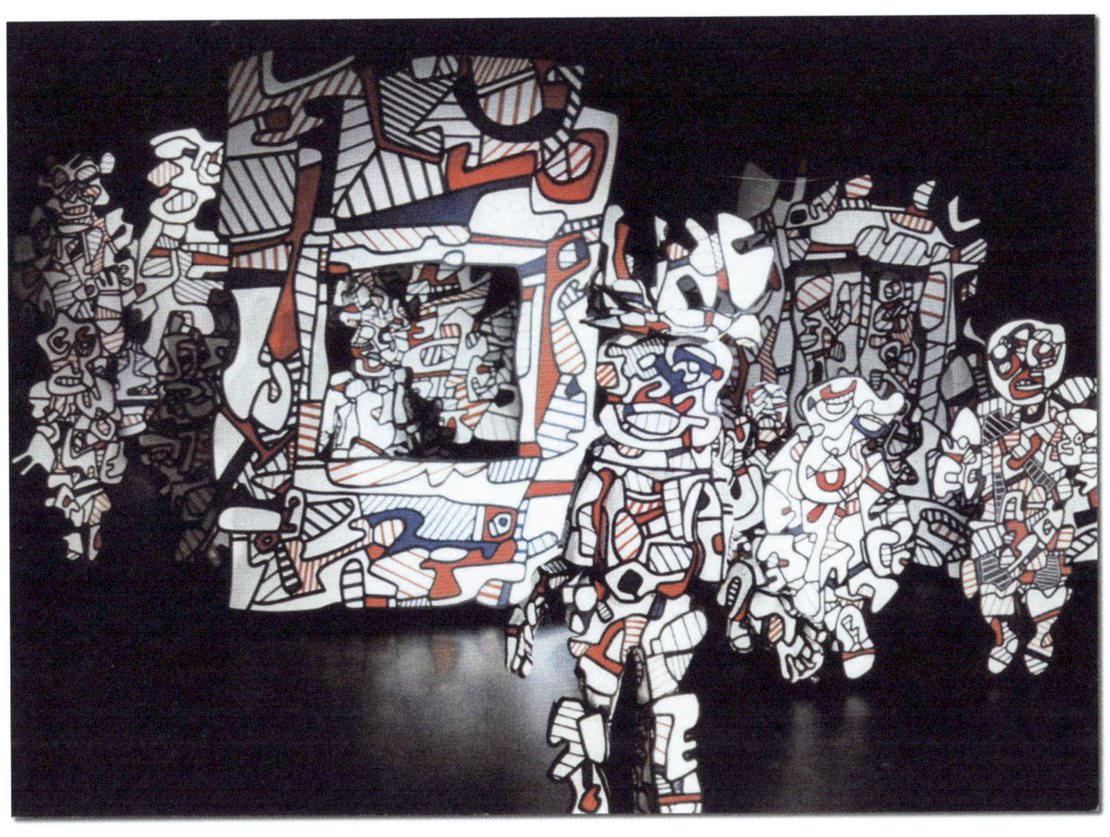

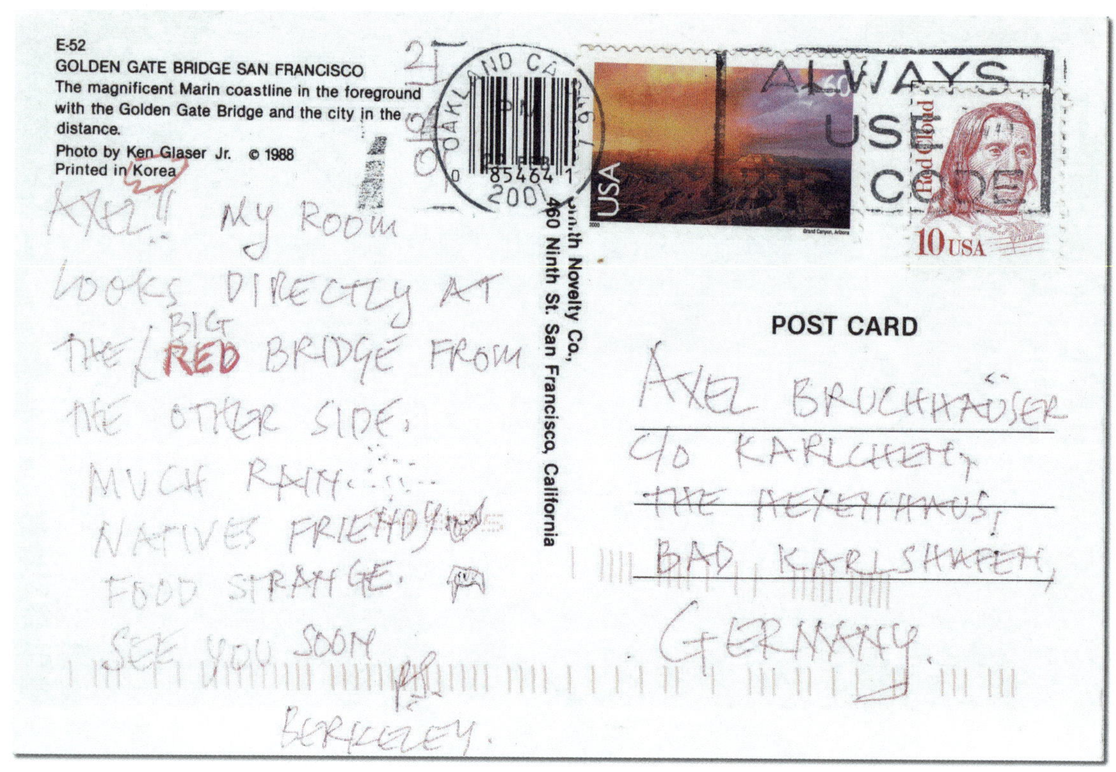
E-52
GOLDEN GATE BRIDGE SAN FRANCISCO
The magnificent Marin coastline in the foreground with the Golden Gate Bridge and the city in the distance.
Photo by Ken Glaser Jr. © 1988
Printed in Korea

Smith Novelty Co., 460 Ninth St. San Francisco, California

OAKLAND CA
ALWAYS USE CODE
USA
10 USA
Red Cloud

AXEL!! MY ROOM LOOKS DIRECTLY AT THE BIG RED BRIDGE FROM THE OTHER SIDE. MUCH RAIN. NATIVES FRIENDLY. FOOD STRANGE. SEE YOU SOON
PS. BERKELEY.

POST CARD

AXEL BRUCHHÄUSER
C/O KARLCHEN,
~~THE HEXENHAUS,~~
BAD KARLSHAFEN,
GERMANY.

Peter Smithson, 21 February 2001

21/02/01

AXEL!! MY ROOM LOOKS DIRECTLY AT THE BIG RED [the word "RED" is emphasised in red ink] BRIDGE FROM THE OTHER SIDE. MUCH RAIN [doodle of raindrops]. NATIVES FRIENDLY. FOOD STRANGE. SEE YOU SOON.
PS. BERKELEY

SAN FRANCISCO

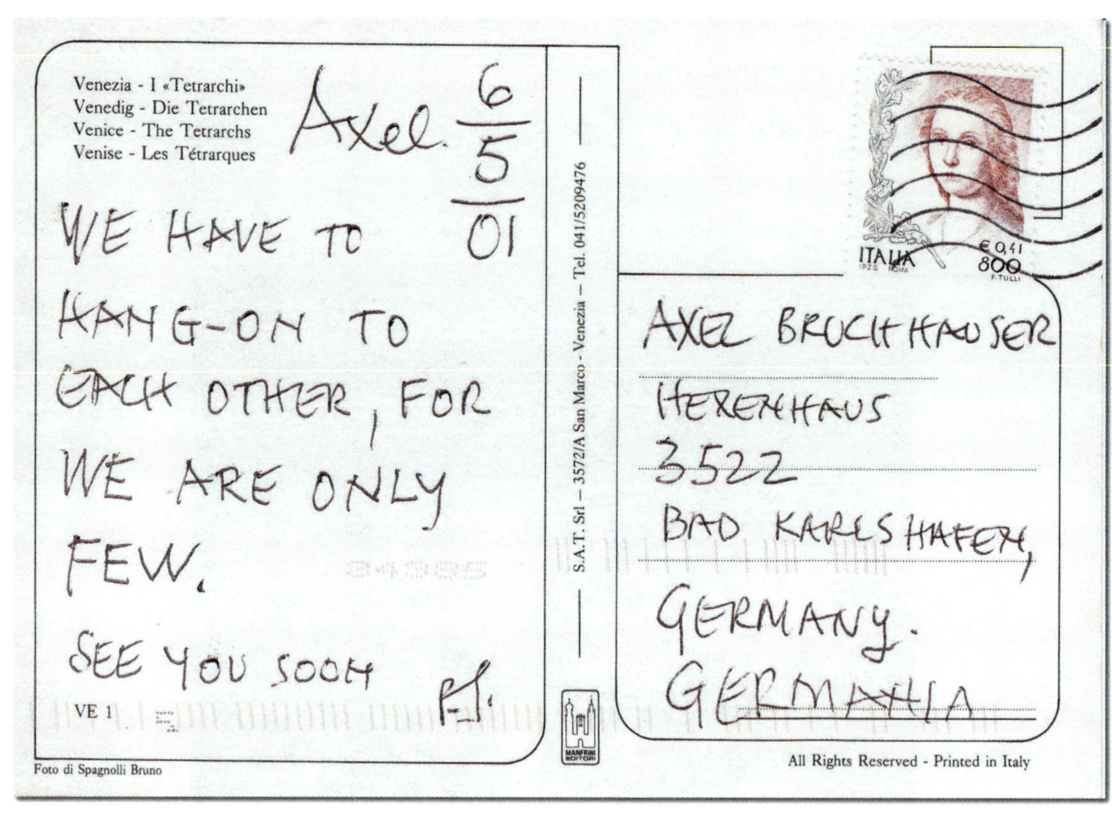
Venezia - I «Tetrarchi»
Venedig - Die Tetrarchen
Venice - The Tetrarchs
Venise - Les Tétrarques

Axel. 6/5/01

WE HAVE TO HANG-ON TO EACH OTHER, FOR WE ARE ONLY FEW.

SEE YOU SOON P.S.

VE 1

Foto di Spagnolli Bruno

S.A.T. Srl — 3572/A San Marco - Venezia — Tel. 041/5209476

ITALIA €0,41 800

AXEL BRUCHHAUSER
HERRENHAUS
3522
BAD KARLSHAFEN,
GERMANY.
GERMANIA

All Rights Reserved - Printed in Italy

Peter Smithson, 6 May 2001

6/5/01

Axel,
WE HAVE TO HANG-ON TO EACH OTHER, FOR WE ARE ONLY FEW.
SEE YOU SOON
P.S.

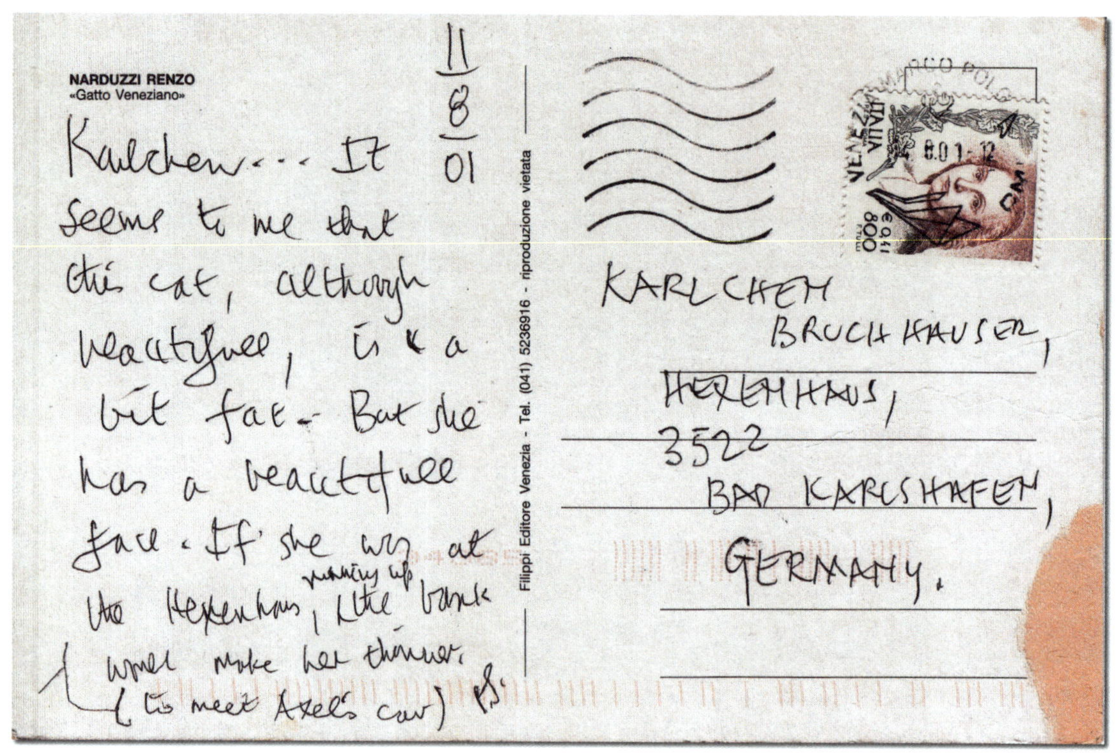

NARDUZZI RENZO
«Gatto Veneziano»

11
8
01

Karlchen... It seems to me that this cat, although beautifull, is a bit fat. But she has a beautifull face. If she was at the Hexenhaus, running up the bank would make her thinner. (to meet Axel's car) PS.

Filippi Editore Venezia - Tel. (041) 5236916 - riproduzione vietata

KARLCHEN
BRUCHHAUSER,
HEXENHAUS,
3522
BAD KARLSHAFEN,
GERMANY.

Peter Smithson, 11 August 2001

11/8/01

Karlchen... It seems to me that this cat, although beautifull, is a bit fat. But she has a beautifull face. If she was at the Hexenhaus, running up the bank (to meet Axel's car) would make her thinner.
PS.

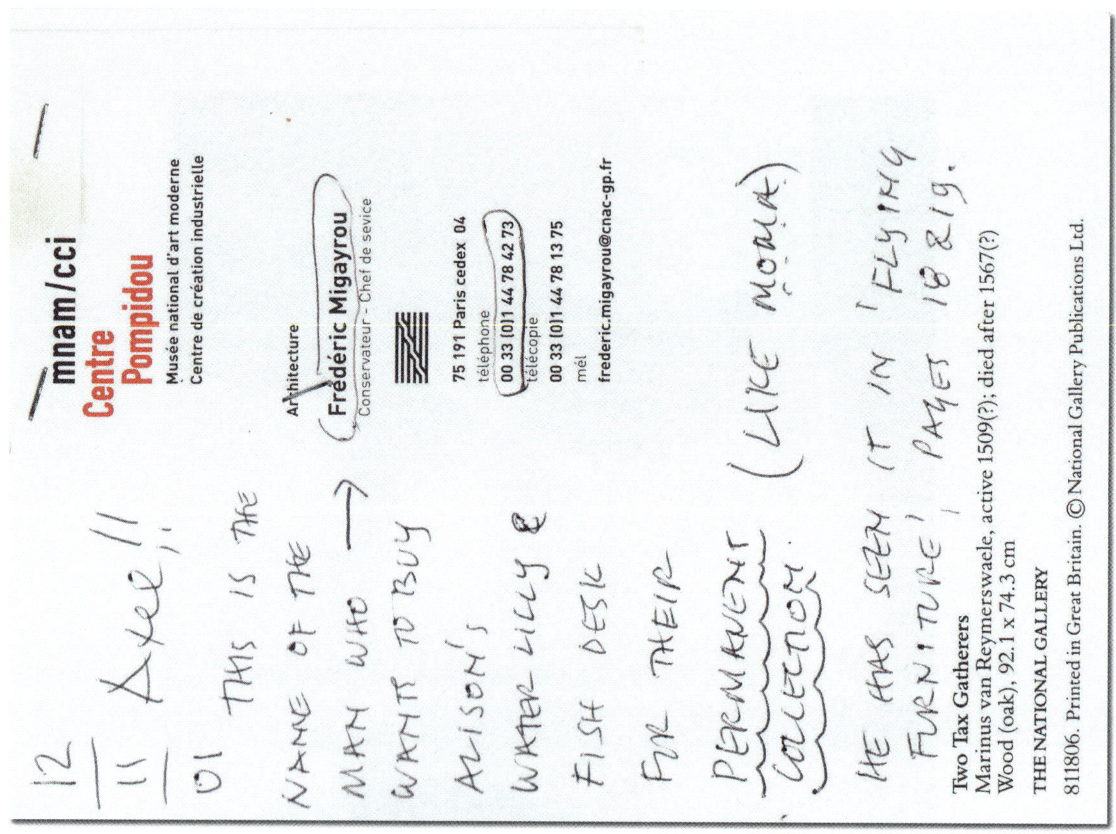

Peter Smithson, 12 November 2001

12/11/01

Axel!!
THIS IS THE NAME OF THE MAN [arrow pointing to Frédéric Migayrou] WHO WANTS TO BUY ALISON'S WATER LILY & FISH DESK FOR THEIR PERMANENT COLLECTION (LIKE MOMA)
HE HAS SEEN IT IN 'FLYING FURNITURE', PAGES 18 & 19.

Unsigned.

See: Smithson, Peter and Unglaub, Karl, *Flying Furniture*, Cologne: Tecta/Verlag der Buchhandlung Walther König, 1999.

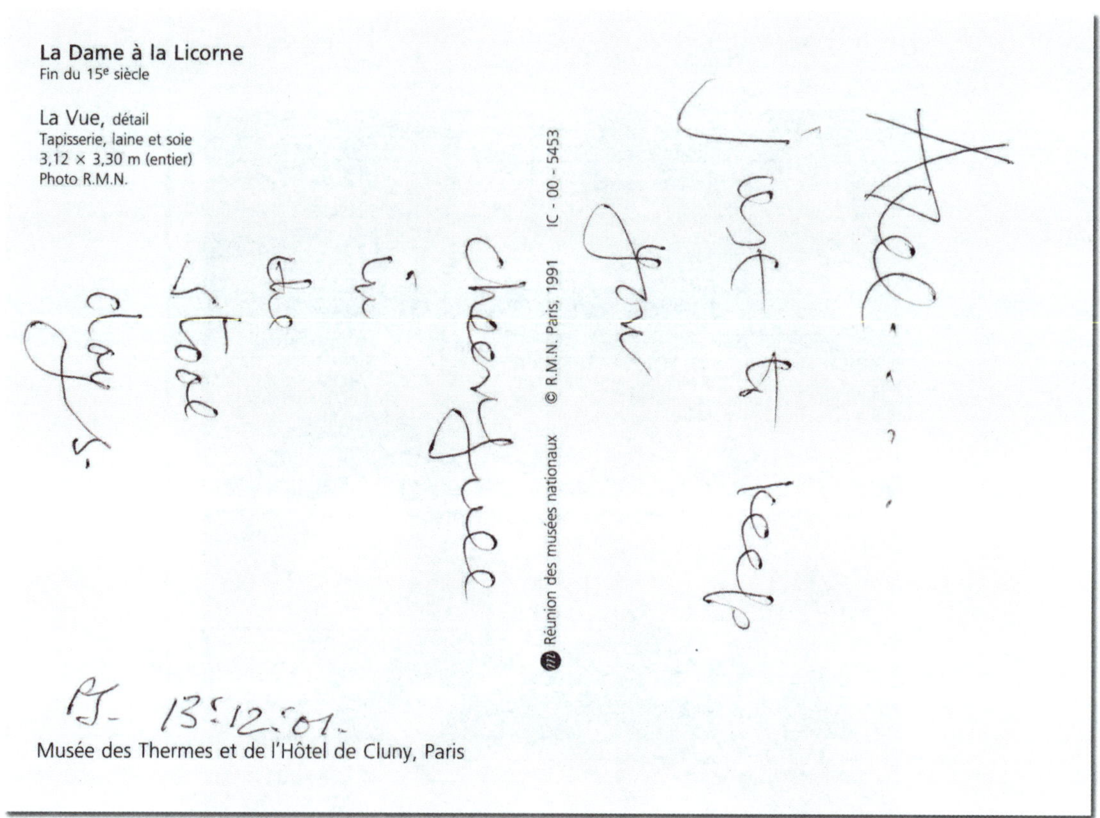

La Dame à la Licorne
Fin du 15e siècle
La Vue, détail
Tapisserie, laine et soie
3,12 × 3,30 m (entier)
Photo R.M.N.
Réunion des musées nationaux © R.M.N. Paris, 1991 IC - 00 - 5453
Musée des Thermes et de l'Hôtel de Cluny, Paris

Peter Smithson, 13 December 2001

Axel....
Just to keep you cheerfull in the stool days.

PS. 13:12:01.

"Stool days" refers to the Cologne furniture fair, which always takes place at the beginning of the year.

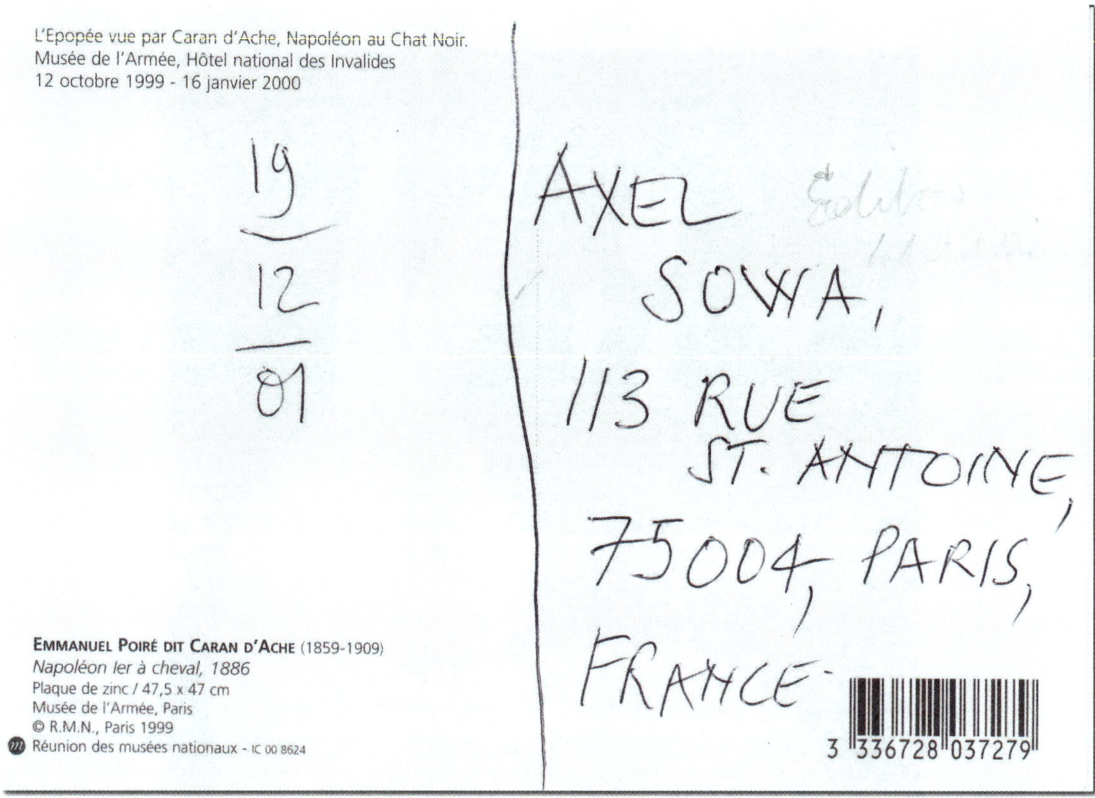

L'Epopée vue par Caran d'Ache, Napoléon au Chat Noir.
Musée de l'Armée, Hôtel national des Invalides
12 octobre 1999 - 16 janvier 2000
19/12/01
AXEL SOWA, 113 RUE ST. ANTOINE, 75004, PARIS, FRANCE.
EMMANUEL POIRÉ DIT CARAN D'ACHE (1859-1909)
Napoléon Ier à cheval, 1886
Plaque de zinc / 47,5 x 47 cm
Musée de l'Armée, Paris
© R.M.N., Paris 1999
Réunion des musées nationaux - IC 00 8624
3 336728 037279

Peter Smithson, 19 December 2001

19/12/01

[Addressed to:]
AXEL SOWA,
113 RUE ST. ANTOINE,
75004, PARIS,
FRANCE

[Written in pencil, probably by Axel Bruchhäuser]: editor *L'Architecture d'Aujourd'hui*

Unsigned.

Axel Sowa was editor-in-chief of *L'Architecture d'Aujourd'hui* journal in Paris from 2000 to 2007. His current research — at University of Aachen, Department of Architectural Theory — is focused on the question of imitation in modern contexts, and on the beginning of the industrial mass-production of building components.

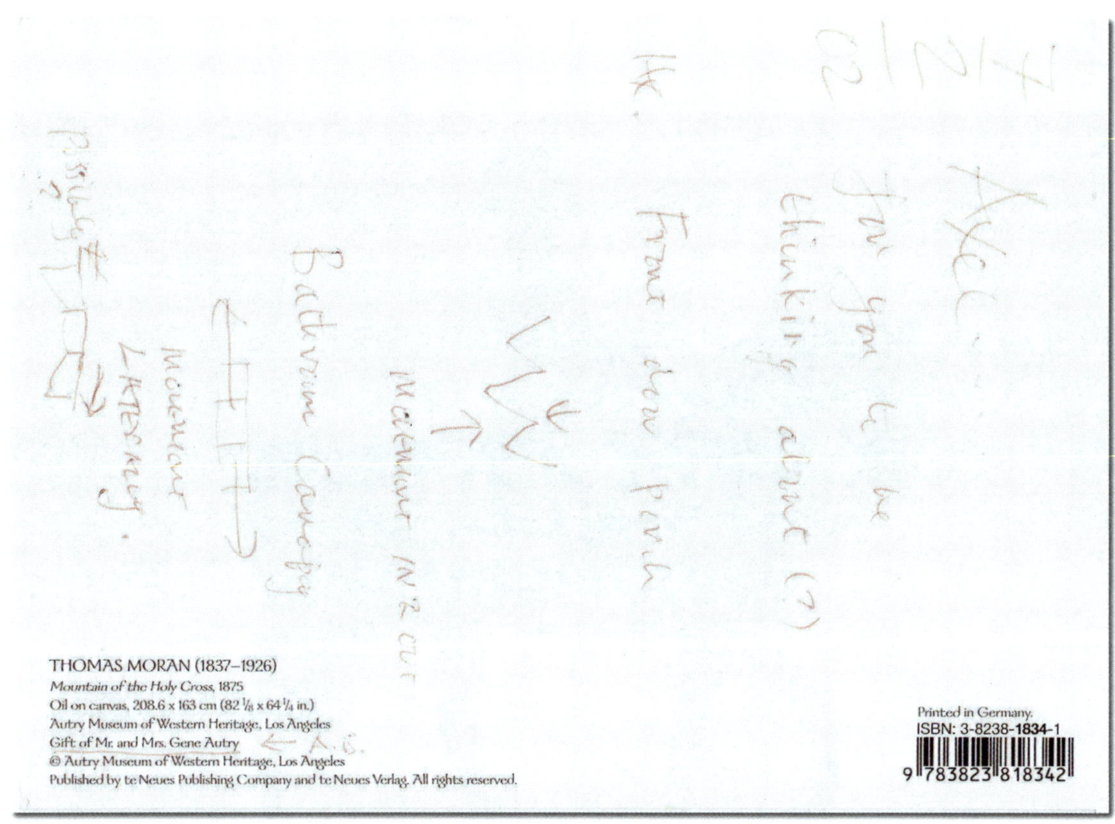

Peter Smithson, 7 February 2002

7/2/02

Axel....
For you to be
thinking about (?)
Hx. Front door porch

[Sketch of a zigzag line, with arrows on both sides and the text]: MOVEMENT IN & OUT

Bathroom Canopy

[Sketch of what could represent roofing for the porch, in three parts, with arrows on both sides and the text]: MOVEMENT LATERALLY

[Sketch of what might be tilted roofing for the porch, in three parts, with arrows on both sides and the text]: Possibly?

Unsigned.

The Hexenhaus Front Door Porch was designed by Peter Smithson in 1998. Several versions were proposed before the final design, which had two doors facing in two different directions; one more obvious and welcoming, another more private and directed to the Hexenbesenraum.

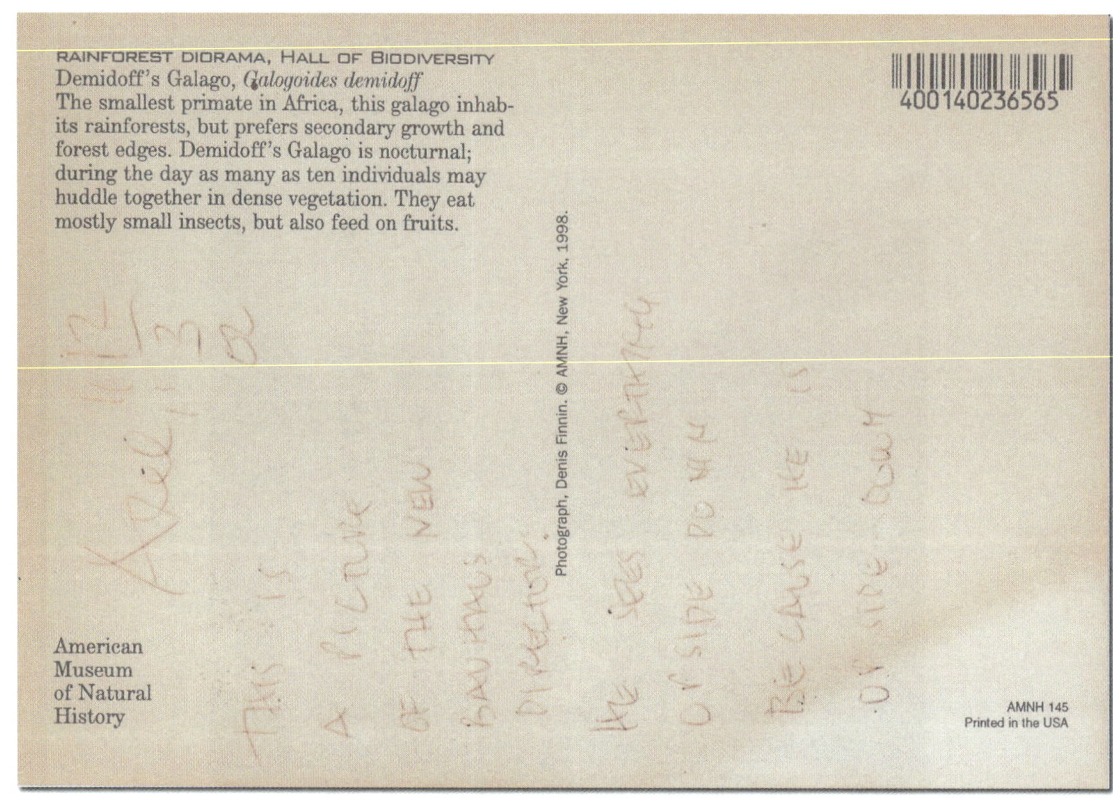
RAINFOREST DIORAMA, HALL OF BIODIVERSITY
Demidoff's Galago, *Galogoides demidoff*
The smallest primate in Africa, this galago inhabits rainforests, but prefers secondary growth and forest edges. Demidoff's Galago is nocturnal; during the day as many as ten individuals may huddle together in dense vegetation. They eat mostly small insects, but also feed on fruits.

400140236565

Photograph, Denis Finnin. © AMNH, New York, 1998.

American Museum of Natural History

AMNH 145
Printed in the USA

Peter Smithson, 12 March 2002

12/3/02

Axel!!

THIS IS
A PICTURE
OF THE NEW
BAUHAUS
DIRECTOR.
HE SEES EVERYTHING
UPSIDE DOWN
BECAUSE HE IS
UP SIDE DOWN.

Unsigned.

After the reunification of Germany, Omar Akbar was the controversial new director of the Bauhaus Dessau Foundation (1998-2009).

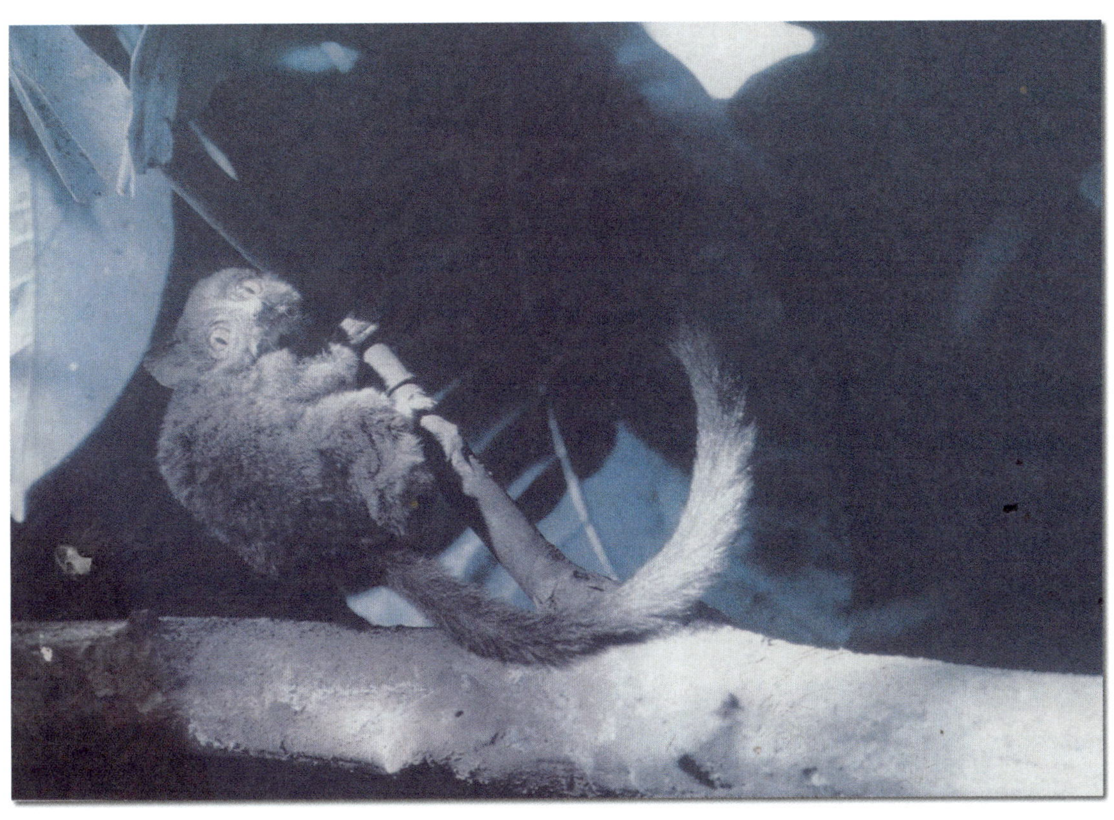

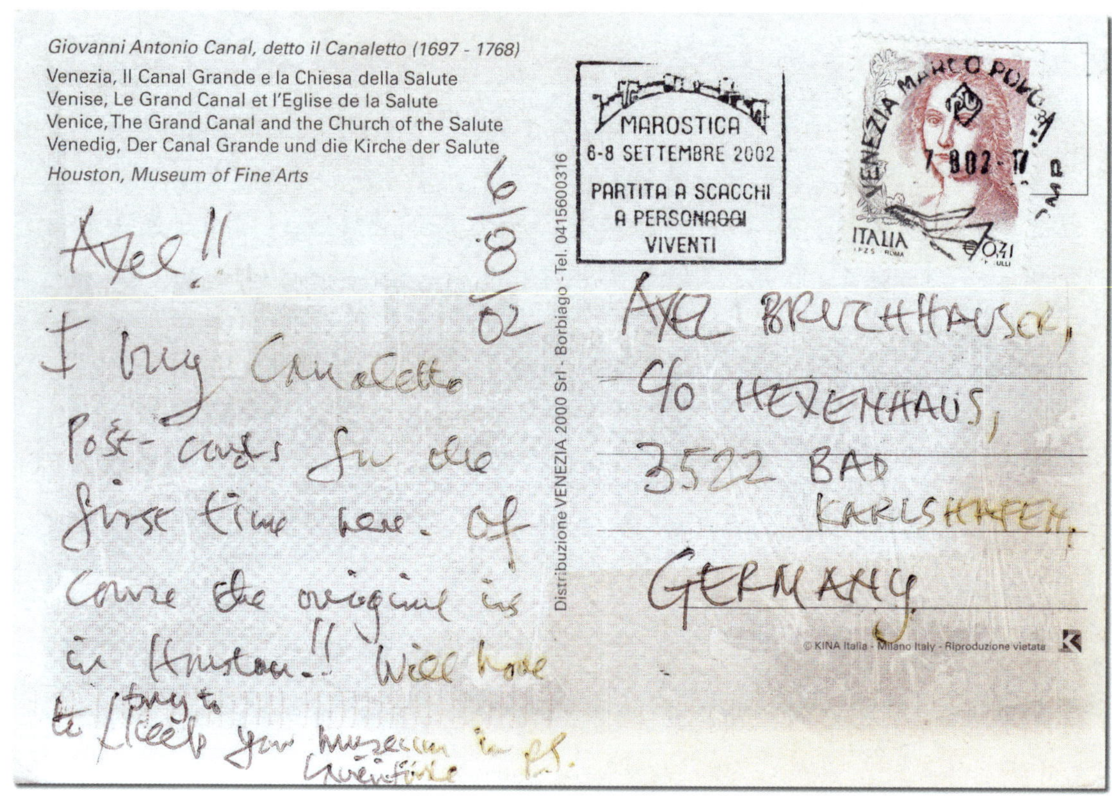

Peter Smithson, 6 August 2002

6/8/02

Axel!!
I buy Canaletto post-cards for the first time here. Of course the original is in Houston!! Will have to try to keep your museum in Lauenförde.
P.S.

The Tecta Kragstuhlmuseum (i.e. the Cantilever Chair Museum) was built, according to Peter Smithson's design, next to the Tecta factory in Lauenförde. It was completed after Peter's death (on 3 March 2003).

This book owes its existence to Axel Bruchhäuser, who generously opened up the Hexenhaus and its treasures, and assisted in tracing all the postcards. His insights were key to understanding the veiled stories and individuals behind this one-sided correspondence.

I am also grateful to Soraya and Simon Smithson, who helped decipher their parents' handwriting and secret codes.

Karlchen IV stepping on the postcards
© Anna Bach, 2018